London's VICTORIA EMBANKMENT

INCLUDING WESTMINSTER BRIDGE, HUNGERFORD BRIDGE, WATERLOO BRIDGE AND BLACKFRIARS BRIDGE

Robert J. Harley

CAPITAL HISTORY

The Thames Embankment is a very beautiful piece of work, and deserving of all praise. Only those who inspect it from an engineering and architectural point of view can appreciate the difficulties that had to be overcome in its construction, and the skill with which the works have been perfected. In the opinion of all engineers, both English and foreign, there has never been so colossal a work in granite put together with the same completeness . . . ***The Graphic, 1868.***

First published 2005

ISBN 185414 284 4

Capital History is an imprint
of Capital Transport Publishing,
P.O. Box 250, Harrow, Middlesex
www.capitaltransport.com

Printed by CS Graphics, Singapore.

CONTENTS

It took some years before Cleopatra's Needle was transported from the shores of the Mediterranean to the banks of the Thames in 1878, the project being plagued by funding difficulties.

CLEOPATRA'S NEEDLE, ALEXANDRIA, PRESENTED TO ENGLAND BY MEHEMET ALI PASHA, BEING EXAMINED BY SIR JAMES ALEXANDER

Introduction

and Acknowledgements

VICTORIA EMBANKMENT, known simply to Londoners as '*The Embankment*', has been a feature of the metropolitan scene since 1869. In summer, when the trees lining the carriageway are in full leaf, the vista is one of a stately riverside avenue, worthy of comparison with other gracious thoroughfares in capital cities such as Paris and Moscow. In historical terms, Victoria Embankment is a relative newcomer – roads such as Whitehall, the Strand and Fleet Street have a greater pedigree and have received more attention from authors, artists and guidebook writers.

This book is an attempt to redress the balance by presenting a series of impressions of the street throughout the years of its existence. The reader is taken on a journey into the past, using various forms of transport to cover the distance from the Houses of Parliament to the edge of the City of London. Whilst writing this account, it became apparent that it was impossible to disentangle the life and history of the Embankment from the two main feeder bridges spanning the Thames at Westminster and Blackfriars. Nor could I omit Waterloo Bridge and Hungerford Bridge, which serves Charing Cross Station.

My first memories of the Embankment come from a visit made in the late 1950s – I was intrigued by the 'hole' in one of the arches of Waterloo Bridge, where trams had once entered the legendary Kingsway Subway. Unfortunately, my handwritten letter to London Transport at 55 Broadway, asking whether any of these fascinating vehicles were still concealed under the bridge behind the shuttering, evinced no response! Such were the frustrations of a juvenile enthusiast in those days. Thankfully, this present work has not encountered any similar problems.

Many of the literary sources I have consulted are listed in the Select Bibliography at the end of the book. I have also been ably assisted by a number of individuals who have freely given of their time and expertise. My gratitude goes to Tom Lee who supplied most of the facts and figures about steamboat operation on the Thames. Dr Gerald Druce very kindly read through the manuscript and offered helpful suggestions. Rosy Thacker and Glynn Wilton of the John Price Memorial Library at the Crich Tramway Village managed to locate much information on the tramways and underground railways serving the Embankment. Photographic views included in this book have come from the collections of C. Carter, John Gent, John Gillham, Ken Glazier, John Meredith, David Packer and D. A. Ruddom.

As always, I record my thanks to my publisher, Jim Whiting.

Chapter 1 THE GRAND VISION

WHEN STANDING on the present day Victoria Embankment, it is very difficult to imagine the scene in pre-Roman days. The Thames was ever subject to the vagaries of wind, weather and tides, and for many centuries the banks of the river were ill defined. Sometimes the breadth of water dividing dry land expanded to over half a mile. No wonder there were few crossing places and little habitation at this location. Primitive port facilities for the embryonic settlement of Londinium began to appear around AD50. The construction of the first London Bridge gave a further impetus to urban development on the north side of the Thames. The bridge provided a vital trade link from the hinterland of the expanding province of Britannia to harbours on the English Channel.

By Saxon times the inhabitants of Lundenwic were already using a trackway to the west of the old city walls. Many folk would have followed the course of the Strand towards Edward the Confessor's new Abbey near the River Tyburn at Westminster, which was dedicated in December 1065.

Floods were an ever present menace and it is recorded that in 1294 a large part of Southwark was inundated. Navigation on the Thames was important in maintaining commercial routes, but the inconvenience caused by high tides presented a barrier to cross-London traffic. Clearly, action had to be taken to stabilise the situation, so that links between Lambeth and Southwark on the south bank and Westminster and Whitehall on the north could be improved. Land reclamation to prevent

The Venetian artist, Giovanni Antonio Canaletto (1697–1768), lived and worked in London from 1746 to 1755. After his arrival, one of his first creative endeavours was to paint this view through one of the arches of Westminster Bridge. As can be seen, the bridge was still under construction at the time. Looking beyond the various small boats and river craft, we can observe the eighteenth century waterfront of the Thames prior to the building of Victoria Embankment.

flooding was dependent on the construction of raised and reinforced earthworks, which needed constant maintenance. Already in late medieval times, a wooden palisade embankment probably protected the stretch of the north bank of the Thames from the mouth of the Fleet River to the waterfront at St Stephen's Chapel by Westminster Hall.

In the sixteenth century some thirty large dwellings, amongst them Arundel House and Somerset House, were built along the Strand. This Tudor property boom set in motion a process of steady urbanisation. By 1529, Henry VIII had appropriated Cardinal Wolsey's York House, renaming it the Palace of Whitehall, and this area of London was destined to become the centre of imperial power with stately buildings to match.

The commerce of this part of the capital was heavily dependent on the river, especially when roads became impassable in winter. Unfortunately an opportunity was missed after the Great Fire of 1666 to implement the master plan of Sir Christopher Wren (1632–1723), which would have transformed London's thoroughfares and would have provided a stone built embankment protecting the north bank of the Thames. As it was, City landowners thwarted the dream of the nation's most famous architect and the scheme never got off the ground. The reality was that wharves, landing stages and makeshift wooden jetties had appeared almost at random along the waterfront to cater for all ranks of society from the monarch downwards. Shipments of hay and comestibles were landed for the new Hungerford Market, opened in 1680. Cross-river passenger traffic relied on a number of ferries. It is estimated there were around thirty separate landing places between the City and the southern end of Whitehall, where boats could be boarded to make the trip across the water. Understandably, the operators of these ferries were among the most vociferous opponents of fixed river crossings. They lobbied hard against the new Westminster Bridge, which was begun in 1739 and completed in 1750. At the other end of the future Victoria Embankment, the Lord Mayor of London laid the foundation stone of Blackfriars Bridge on 31st October 1760 and the finished structure opened in 1769.

Another function of the River Thames was to provide drinking water to various parts of the capital. Private companies engaged in this activity loudly trumpeted the health giving properties of their water supply. This stance mirrored contemporary beliefs, which failed to associate the spread of disease with polluted drinking water. In 1847 a Royal Commission was set up to examine ways of improving London's housing, streets and sanitation. The result of one of its recommendations was the formation of the Metropolitan Sewers Commission. Unfortunately, the authorities at the time lacked the medical knowledge and the organisational know-how to produce a coherent policy on pollution and disease control. The general situation was exacerbated after 1847, when Parliament decreed that domestic and industrial drainage should be diverted from some 30,000 cesspools into sewers which discharged directly into the Thames.

Two major outbreaks of cholera in 1848/49 and 1853/54 caused around 25,000 fatalities in the capital. In July 1855, the celebrated scientist, Michael Faraday, remarked on the lamentable state of the Thames in a letter to THE TIMES:

> *. . . the appearance and smell of the water forced themselves upon my attention. The whole of the river was an opaque, pale brown fluid . . . The smell was very bad, and common to the whole of the water; the whole river was for the time a real sewer . . .*

Not surprisingly, since the situation remained unchecked, the River Thames continued to stink, and the smell got so bad that, by the summer of 1859, a total of 4,281 tons of chalk lime, 50 tons of carbolic acid and 478 tons of chloride of lime had to be heaped into the stagnant channel in an attempt to mitigate some of the worst effects of the pollution. Whilst all this was going on, the incidence of water-borne disease increased amongst the population. It seemed to many concerned individuals – social campaigners and some Members of Parliament – that no decisive action would ever be taken to solve the unpleasant situation.

However, on the credit side, the Victorian era could engender a positive atmosphere, when science and engineering were applied to tackle previously insurmountable problems. Collectively, over many centuries, the planners of London had been trying to improve the face of the capital – with varying degrees of success. Schemes had come and gone; some of them were implemented, while others failed through want of interest or lack of finance.

The traditional British deference to property rights and the intransigence of vested interests scuppered many promising ideas – most notably the imaginative rebuilding plans after the Great Fire of 1666. The ability to improve transport facilities had been further handicapped by a lack of a comprehensive overview of the situation, the unwillingness of financial institutions to invest in long-term solutions, and the insularity of London's planners, who failed to learn lessons from successful projects overseas.

Victoria Embankment can be cited as an example of one grand project seen through to fruition. As a conduit for a major outfall sewer it contributed in no small measure to the eradication of water-borne disease. It also drastically altered part of the waterfront of the River Thames, and it inspired other designs for new roads, bridges, buildings and public monuments.

As early as 1840, the Metropolitan Improvement Commission had lobbied Parliament in support of a Thames Embankment from Westminster to Blackfriars. The scheme incurred the opposition of wharf owners and provoked a negative response from the City authorities. However, the idea had taken root and over the next two decades the plans reappeared in various guises. Elevated roadways on both sides of the Thames were projected. They would have been supported on cast iron arches, which would have allowed river craft and barges access to the various wharves at high tide. The aesthetics of these plans were rather marred by the inclusion of cranes and landing stages, which would have obscured parts of the ornamental highway. Luckily, the capital was to be spared this unfortunate marriage of docking facilities and elegant avenues!

The need for any sort of commercial activity, especially on the Westminster side of the river, was questionable, bearing in mind the drastic changes taking place in the nation's transport system. The opening of the West India Docks in 1802 began a shift of much commercial activity away from the traditional geographical heart of metropolitan life. The establishment of the Port of London and the construction of further docks rendered many small wharves uneconomic.

Then there were the railways. It is recorded that the first shipment by rail of coal to London arrived in 1845. From then on, steady progress was made in giving customers what they wanted – an efficient and convenient method of getting freight and passengers from point A to point B – and the transport of goods by means of the River Thames suffered accordingly. Merchants and utility companies relocated their warehouses and depots so as to take advantage of the expanded railway layout.

In spite of these financial trends, some smaller wharves on the South Bank of the river managed to survive well into the twentieth century, but on the Westminster side of the water a solid embankment wall unencumbered by quay openings and tidal pools was the order of the day. This recommendation was endorsed by the Royal Commission on the Thames Embankment which examined the situation in 1861. After questioning a host of interested parties, it was decided to authorise the Metropolitan Board of Works to commence detailed preparations for the construction work. The MBW was established as a direct result of some bold thinking on behalf of the Government of Mr Disraeli, which saw the need for a new body to oversee affairs in the capital. The Board came into being on 1st January 1856, and it lasted until 1889, when its functions were transferred to the newly-created London County Council.

Parliament also gave permission for taxes on coal and wine to be levied to raise the capital needed for the project. This reliable source of finance was vital, bearing in mind the financial crisis of 1857, which effectively delayed private investment in many large scale projects – and, as it turned out, it was a farsighted move, because the next disaster was just around the corner, when in May 1866, the banking collapse of Overend, Gurney caused major disruption to the financial markets.

As might have been expected, competing ideas were submitted to the Commission. Many failed to find favour. One scheme envisaged the transformation of a tract of reclaimed land between Hungerford Bridge and Waterloo Bridge. Contemporary drawings detail a wonderful arrangement of terraces, ornamental balustrades, stairways and fountains that would have led down to the Thames. A line of shops was also included – potentially, the only such facilities along the whole thoroughfare. This flight of fancy was predictably brought down to earth by the objections of a neighbouring aristocratic landowner.

In the mid-Victorian era there was a three-pronged attack on the status quo. London needed to respond to the demands of aesthetes, the needs of capitalism and commerce, and the wishes of philanthropists and social reformers. In the first category there existed a widespread desire to beautify the main thoroughfares – to create in London what had been achieved in Paris.

Across the Channel, Georges Eugène, Baron Haussmann (1809–1891), had transformed the capital city of France. Broad boulevards and splendid new buildings had resulted in Paris being a centre of pilgrimage for architects and engineers from Europe and America. However, hero worship of foreigners has never been a strong point of the British Establishment. Some of the Baron's creations were simply deemed unsuitable for adoption in the capital city of the Empire. Critics were quick to pour cold water on the idea that London should ape its Gallic neighbour. It was widely reported in the British press that, through the autocratic machinations of Napoleon III and Baron Haussmann, some 27,000 buildings had been flattened to accommodate the new streets. Added to this wanton demolition was the notion that wide pavements supporting a 'café culture' might appear in staid areas like Westminster – all of which was anathema to the prudish Victorians. After all, Messrs Gladstone & Co. knew very well what went on in Parisian society!

While the French could laud Baron Haussmann and his achievements, a relatively unsung hero, in the person of George John Vulliamy (1817–1886), was studiously producing plans for the new Thames embankments. Vulliamy was appointed chief architect to the Metropolitan Board of Works and worked closely with Bazalgette and Sir John Thwaites. Although subject to conflicting advice as to which architectural style to adopt, Vulliamy managed to avoid some of the uglier excesses of Victorian design, and the clear, uncluttered shape of today's Victoria Embankment owes much to his skill and foresight.

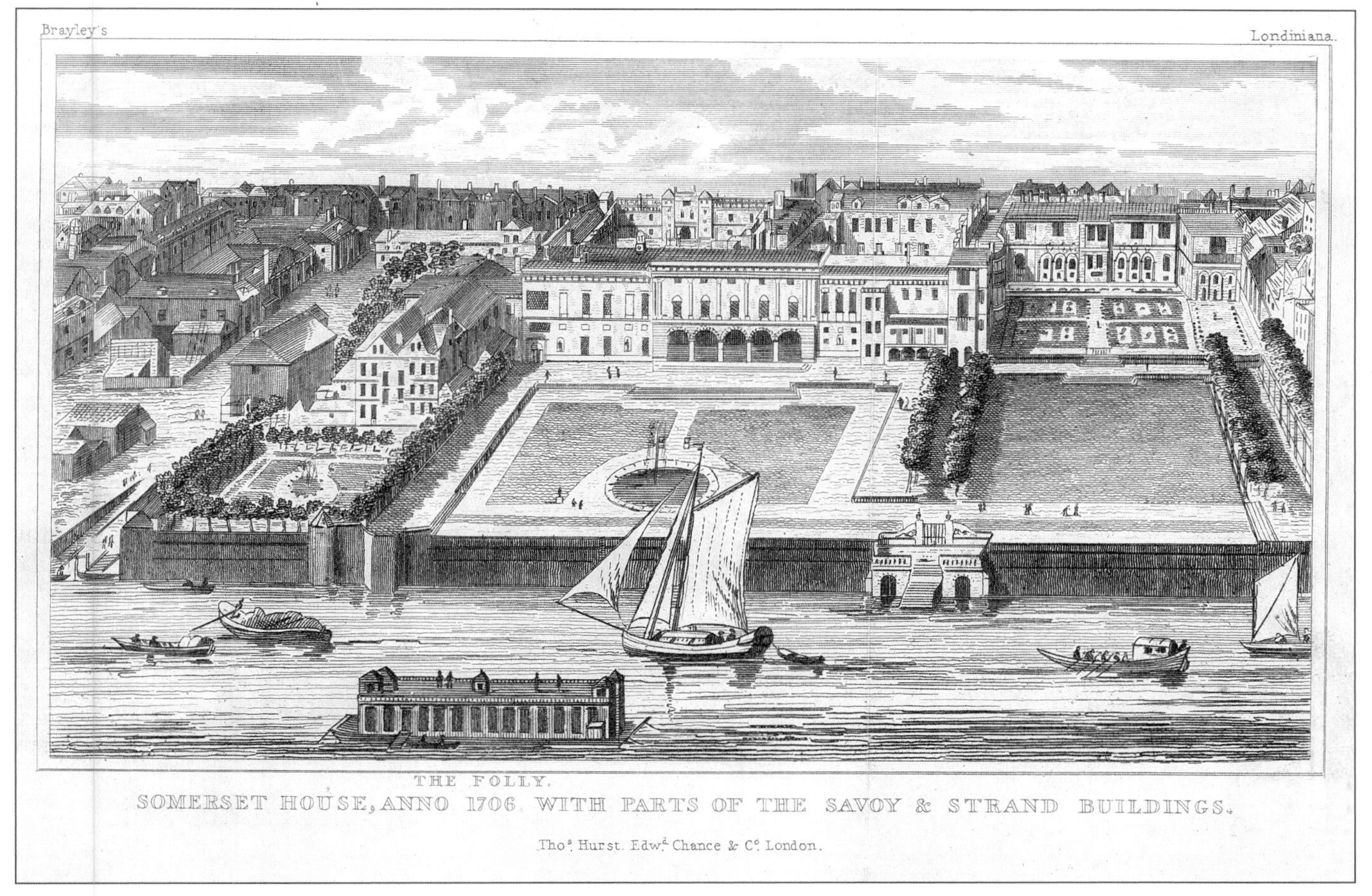

Brayley's
Londiniana.
THE FOLLY.
SOMERSET HOUSE, ANNO 1706, WITH PARTS OF THE SAVOY & STRAND BUILDINGS.
Thos. Hurst. Edwd. Chance & Co. London.

This lively scene, dated 1706, shows the original Somerset House with parts of the Savoy and Strand Buildings. Note the contrast between the elegant landing stage with ornamental gate and the more functional slipway to the left of the picture. Somerset House was later rebuilt nearer the Thames and was extended with a Palladian style façade. The traffic on the river seems fairly routine, with the exception of the floating 'Folly' in midstream.

The whole Thames Embankment scheme would eventually lead to a vast engineering enterprise that included the construction of the Albert, Victoria and Chelsea embankments. The new road from Westminster Bridge to Blackfriars Bridge was conceived as one of the main arteries of an intercepting system of storm relief and wastewater conduits to transport effluent away from the centre of the metropolis. By means of gravity and an auxiliary pumping station at Abbey Mills in West Ham, the contents of the Northern Outfall Sewer would eventually reach a large, powerful pumping station at Beckton. Here on the Essex bank of the Thames, at a safe distance from the centre of town, steam driven engines would expel London's liquid detritus into the river, and thus the unwanted sewage would be swept out to sea. A similar facility at Crossness was planned for the Kent side to cater for wastewater carried by the Southern Outfall Sewer.

The man at the helm was Joseph William Bazalgette (1819–1891). He was born at Enfield and, at the age of seventeen, began his apprenticeship as a civil engineer. He established his own civil engineering practice in 1842, and later worked with the Metropolitan Sewers Commission. On 25th January 1856, he was appointed Chief Engineer to the Metropolitan Board of Works at a salary of £1,000 per annum – a handsome sum in those days. Equally impressive were the names of the three professional referees who submitted testimonials in his favour – I. K. Brunel, Robert Stephenson and William Cubitt.

Bazalgette quickly set about reforming his department and surrounding himself with capable assistants. For the supervision of London's main drainage, which would include preliminary work on the Thames Embankment, he employed two surveyors, five clerks, twenty draughtsmen, twenty-two sewer engineers, and no fewer than fifty-nine clerks of works to be present on site in all weathers in order to ensure that labourers and contractors adhered to the high standards expected of them. In short, Bazalgette restructured what was essentially a public, governmental institution along efficient lines more commonly associated with thriving commercial enterprises. His single minded devotion to hard work would ensure that the recommendations of the Royal Commission and the resultant provisions of the 1863 Act of Parliament were carried out to a successful conclusion.

As part of the canvassing for the building of the Embankment, a number of watercolours were produced and printed showing possible designs. Two alternative steam boat landing piers at Waterloo Bridge are shown here. Neither was built. Guildhall Library

Below **Ornate landing stairs for boats between Hungerford and Waterloo bridges are envisaged in this view, with ornamental gardens on the roof of the single-storey building opposite.** Guildhall Library

Bottom **A proposed remodelling of York Gate which, in common with all the other ideas on this double page spread, failed to be realised. Changes in architectural taste and money problems put paid to such imperial-looking extravagances illustrated.** Guildhall Library

The preamble to the official legislation owes much to Bazalgette's forthright style; it shows a marked change of attitude when compared to previous attempts:

The Commissioners of Her Majesty's Works and Public Buildings may embank and fill up the Bed and Shore of the River Thames as shown on the aforesaid Plans, and may pull down and remove any Buildings, Stairs, Piers, Landing Places, Hards, Piles, or other Erections on the prescribed Lands, and may construct thereon such Embankment, Stairs, Piers, and Landing Places, Buildings, and Works, and do all such Things as may in their Opinion be necessary or expedient in order to carry into effect the Purposes of this Act . . .

Right **One proposal was for a raised roadway that would have retained access to the various wharfs that existed in the path of the Embankment.**

Below **The title of this 1881 engraving, *The Thames Embankment As It Might Be – A Suggestive Sketch*, implies that this scene rightly belongs in the *Castles in the Air* category. The actual thoroughfare had been open barely ten years and plans were obviously afoot to beautify, ennoble and generally enhance Bazalgette's original. At first glance, a view such as this could not fail to enchant the Victorian middle classes – it is the epitome of good order and decorum – but to modern eyes it looks so terribly staged that the whole thing is barely credible! This is an idealised world where, in the August Bank Holiday sunshine, the band entertains the passers-by, all of whom seem to have just stepped out of a fashion catalogue. In one respect, the unknown artist was remarkably prescient – the retired wooden fighting ship, now converted to a café, would return at the end of the twentieth century in the guise of the floating pub/restaurant.**

Work has finally started. A report of 6th September 1862 describes the event depicted here: *Several barges were moored in the river, immediately opposite the newly erected mansion of the Duke of Buccleuch, and gangs of labourers have since been busily employed in driving piles into the bed of the river.* It is worth noting that the Duke of Buccleuch's Montagu House was completed in 1864 and possessed a garden, which ran all the way to the banks of the Thames. The noble aristocrat received handsome compensation for the strip of land he had to give up to facilitate the construction of Victoria Embankment.

THE

THAMES EMBANKMENT.

DRIVING THE FIRST PILE.

AMONGST the many gossiping anecdotes told by Horace Walpole that most frequently remembered is the epigrammatic retort which was made by his father, Sir Robert, when Prime Minister, to good Queen Anne. One of the many whims and fancies which entered the head of that good-hearted lady was that of enlarging the private gardens and grounds of St. James's Palace to such an extent that the adjoining park would have been very seriously curtailed. She very naturally consulted her Prime Minister, asking him, in the first place, how much the alteration would cost. "Only three crowns," said Sir Robert with marked emphasis. The Queen took the hint, and the scheme was abandoned.

Latterly with us a much more important work was very nearly spoiled, and for some time interrupted, not by the Sovereign, but by a Duke, who had possessed himself of some Government leases, and the battle of the "Thames Embankment," memorable for the mistakes of a Secretary of State and the imperturbable good humour and pluck of the Prime Minister, was fought out with considerable skill and much acerbity. The popular side gained; and the Duke of Buccleuch, if he should ever inhabit his new house, will have the mortification of seeing omnibuses and waggons pass along the road between his ducal presence and the silent highway. We must own, however, that the Duke, when he could no longer withstand, yielded with a good grace. We have already had Portland-place spoiled by the whim of a noble lady whose house is now being converted into a gigantic hotel, and London could not possibly afford to be made more ugly than it is. The splendid new bridge at Westminster, the new Palaces of Parliament, and the Thames embankment are works of combined utility and architectural beauty which will go far to redeem us from an utter deadness to the beauty of our gigantic city; and when the embankment is finished, running as it will from Pimlico to Blackfriars-bridge, and beyond it, the relief to the crowded Strand and Fleet-street will be enormous.

A commencement has been made with this important undertaking. On Wednesday and Thursday, last week, several barges were moored in the river, immediately opposite the newly-erected mansion of the Duke of Buccleuch, and gangs of labourers have since been busily employed in driving piles into the bed of the river. It is said to be the intention to bring into operation the steam-windlass for working the "monkey," or pile-driving machine, by which a great saving is effected, both in time and manual labour. Those windlasses may be seen daily at work in driving the piles at the works of the new railway-bridge now erecting on the eastern side of Blackfriars-bridge.

In order words, the lethargy of the past was to be swept aside by the powers granted by Parliament. It was hoped that urban regeneration would then follow on a substantial scale.

Although not as flamboyant a character as his contemporary, Isambard Kingdom Brunel, Joseph William Bazalgette and his achievements merit comparison with the best the nineteenth century can offer. He has been credited as effecting a total change in metropolitan planning by his 'professional managerial style'. It has been said that he, more than any other Victorian engineer, marks the change between the self taught 'amateur' of previous decades, who often relied on trial and error to achieve results, and the professional civil engineer we know today, whose training and competence is backed up by qualifications and a sound knowledge of his métier.

Bazalgette's mental tenacity was coupled with an astute perception of contemporary politics and an understanding of whom to cultivate in order to get things done. He had already proved himself an able performer when it came to testifying before House of Commons' Select Committees. He came to be regarded as an 'expert witness', who would later confirm this

As a contrast to the 1862 view, steam power has now come to the aid of the contractors employed in pile driving. This formidable machine appeared in the Illustrated London News for 5th May 1866. It was acquired in order to speed up the work, and was said to cut 'from thirty to forty piles in a day'. Perhaps the fine spring weather has brought out all the sightseers in the picture.

accolade by tirelessly submitting detailed plans, drawings and reference documents to Parliament for inclusion in the relevant construction Bills. In recognition of his many achievements, Bazalgette was knighted in 1874.

Sir Joseph's prowess is commemorated on the Embankment by a monument erected to celebrate the completion of the project. It contains the inscription in Latin – *flumini vincula posuit – he placed chains on the river*. This tribute sums up only part of the work of a great engineer; he was also active in other areas of metropolitan life. His career would encompass numerous improvements to London's streets and bridges. He was involved in the rebuilding of Hammersmith Bridge; he supervised the reconstruction of Putney Bridge and oversaw the work on the new Battersea Bridge, which opened in 1890. He was instrumental in completing slum clearance projects and he acted as adviser for many sanitation schemes at home and abroad. He was remarkably prescient when he suggested, as early as 1878, the need for a new bridge near the Tower of London, a tunnel under the Thames at Blackwall and a ferry at Woolwich. In 1884, he was elected President of the Institution of Civil Engineers.

After some delays, the grand project began on 20th July 1864, when Sir John Thwaites, Chairman of the Metropolitan Board of Works, laid the first stone of the Victoria Embankment. Sir John had long favoured the construction of a Thames Embankment in conjunction with the building of a low level

The title for this scene reads – *Progress of the Thames Embankment near Arundel Street, Strand* – and the text continues: *The construction of the Thames Embankment which extends from Waterloo Bridge to the east side of Temple Gardens, a length of 1970ft., is rapidly approaching completion. The illustration shows the progress of the masonry and brickwork which compose the outer wall of the embankment, faced with cut granite, and the arched passages of the drain and subway. The view is taken from the outside verge, looking towards the shore in the direction of the Temple.*

sewer and had lobbied Parliament to achieve this goal. Thwaites had previously served as a metropolitan sewer commissioner and had been originally elected to the MBW as a representative for Southwark and Greenwich. He possessed the determination and managerial skills to direct and control all the disparate elements in the MBW. Contemporaries described him as a solid and dependable man, who could evaluate opposing points of view. He defended the MBW and was loyal to Bazalgette and his other colleagues.

Sir John's lasting legacy to Londoners was his implacable opposition to the commercial exploitation of the new Embankment. He was a member of the 1861 Royal Commission, and he advocated that reclaimed land in Hungerford Reach should be regarded as a public asset, not to be given over to wharf owners, warehouses or retail establishments. In this he had the support of many influential citizens who wanted to maintain the elegance of the new thoroughfare enhanced by gardens and 'noble' stone buildings.

Contracts for the building of Victoria Embankment were initially awarded for two distinct construction sites – the dividing line being situated at Waterloo Bridge – but the late intervention of the Metropolitan District Railway resulted in Bazalgette drawing up a third contract for the section between Temple Gardens and Blackfriars Bridge. Also included in this

This moonlit view of the Blackfriars Bridge end of Victoria Embankment illustrates the frantic activity necessary to finish the construction work. This 'atmospheric' picture is enhanced by the glow of steam engines and braziers, which cast shadows over the gangs of labourers who toil to complete the project. Crowds of homeward bound Londoners have gathered on Blackfriars Bridge to watch.

third contract was a commitment for laying the road surface and maintaining the pavements along the whole Embankment.

The workforce assembled for the task of completing the grand project represented a wide spectrum of building contractors, site engineers, craftsmen, mechanics, skilled workers, boatmen and a large pool of unskilled labourers. According to documents issued by the Metropolitan Board of Works, bricklayers, carpenters, blacksmiths and stonemasons could expect to receive six shillings and sixpence (32p) for ten hours work a day. Labourers collected three shillings and ninepence (18p) a day, whilst excavators earned four shillings and sixpence (22p). Sunday was generally acknowledged as a rest day in the working week, but as the pressure to complete the job mounted, critical reports began to circulate that certain contractors had broken the rules. Predictably, the sabbatarians among the members of the MBW were not amused, and it took the conciliation skills of Bazalgette and his officers to defuse the situation.

Delays due to inclement weather, outbreaks of illness and labour troubles amongst the workers were kept to a minimum. But, even so, the task took longer than the predicted three years originally allowed for the work. One large obstacle to progress proved to be the Blackfriars premises of the City of London Gas, Light & Coke Company. A stream of barges laden with coal served their works near Blackfriars Bridge. The stubbornness of the company officials and their reluctance to relocate caused Bazalgette to redesign the approach to Blackfriars Bridge. Fortunately for posterity, the malodorous gas works and the coal barges were finally evicted, and it was not necessary to rejig the road layout.

It was reported that, by 1869, the contractors, Thomas Brassey and George Furness, were employing around 1,250 workmen on one of their sections of the Victoria Embankment. Engineers and contractors were expected to work to a set of comprehensive drawings and plans. In July 1863, a collection of thirty-four detailed section and elevation drawings was published, together with a further fifty-six pages of specifications.

The retaining wall of the embankment was constructed of bricks faced with granite, and the foundations of the whole structure were firmly embedded in Portland cement. Bazalgette championed this type of cement in the face of misgivings by

This picture was published on the occasion of the opening of the Embankment to pedestrians in July 1868. The contemporary caption reads thus:

'The opening to foot-passengers of the river terrace along the Thames Embankment, from the steamboat pier at Essex Street, Strand, to Westminster Bridge, took place on Thursday week. There was no ceremony . . . After walking along the embankment to the pier at Essex Street, Sir John Thwaites took off his hat, and, standing almost alone, declared the road open. At this signal a salute of guns was fired, and the public were at once admitted to the use of the footway. The party then went on board special steamboats, and so down the river to the Abbey Mills pumping-station at North Woolwich . . . The footway thus opened is beautifully flagged with Yorkshire stone for about two thirds of its length.'

many of his fellow civil engineers. They favoured the traditional mix of 'Roman' cement, citing the argument that the Portland variety was almost twice as expensive and its durability was untested. An assistant engineer on the project, John Grant, was delegated to conduct experiments with a view to using Portland cement throughout the whole drainage scheme. He conducted over three hundred tests on materials supplied by twelve different manufacturers. Grant was meticulous in his task, with the result that his recommendations changed the face of future construction work. He can be credited with pioneering a rigorous form of quality control, which we nowadays take for granted. It was found that Portland cement hardened with age and was actually strengthened by being immersed in water. Both these properties were ideal for the Victoria Embankment and the whole London Outfall Sewer project.

Just over 37 acres (15ha.) of land was reclaimed from the foreshore of the river. Cofferdams of different designs were employed to allow the tidal waters of the river to be excluded

Two views of the Embankment with Somerset House on the left. In the upper view, construction work on the new thoroughfare is nearly finished, with little more to be done than completion of the lamp standards. The building line east of Somerset House will shortly be transformed and the gasworks near Blackfriars will be demolished. In the lower view, new buildings now follow the line of the road and the trees have grown to maturity.

from the construction site. Pile drivers mounted on barges were used to drive in the wooden piles needed to surround each cofferdam. At one stage, George Furness changed methods and experimented with wrought iron caissons, but these were more expensive and time consuming than the traditional wood piling method.

The same contractor also had to put up with the inconvenience of maintaining access to the landing stages at Westminster and Hungerford Bridge. Steamboat passengers had to be shepherded safely from the jetties. Other river vessels, especially those filled with sightseers eager to observe the construction works at first hand, had to be controlled and kept at a safe distance so as not to interfere with vital deliveries of building materials and equipment to the site.

It is not surprising to read that Furness actually claimed to have spent some £87,607 over budget. This cost overrun was covered by the MBW. It is apparent that the presence of Bazalgette as an 'honest broker' between contractors and

Thirty years after the opening, and Victoria Embankment has matured into a graceful, tree lined avenue – just the sort of place to take a midday stroll, away from the hustle and bustle of the main streets of the metropolis. *HMS Buzzard*, here pictured at anchor, adds to the beauty of the scene.

supervising engineers ensured that no major disputes detracted from the final achievement of finishing the roadway and the surrounding embankment.

After completion of the main part of the project, gas lamps, positioned at regular intervals along the Embankment wall, supplied the finishing touches to the thoroughfare. The unusual intertwined dolphin motif had been specially designed by C. H. Mabey; the prototype had been exhibited at the Royal Academy Show of 1863. They were complemented by bronze mooring rings, in the shape of a lion's head, which were placed at twenty feet (6 metre) intervals on the river wall.

A high priority was also given to the planting of trees on either side of the carriageway. The choice of the London Plane to line the thoroughfare was inspired. *Platanus x acerifolia* is a particularly hardy and adaptable species, well suited to the polluted environment of the metropolis. Trees of *Platanus orientalis* were positioned on the landward side of the road at the junction with Horse Guards Avenue.

The first members of the public to enjoy the fruits of the labours of Sir Joseph and his workforce were pedestrians, who, on 30th July 1868, were allowed to use the new footway from Westminster to the Temple. The completed thoroughfare, over a mile and a third (2.09 km) in length and 100 feet (30.4 metres) wide, was officially opened on 13th July 1870. However, this being London, the royal pomp and circumstance was spoilt somewhat by an outbreak of hooliganism!

The setting for the inauguration was regal enough – ornamental pavilions and grandstands were put up to accommodate the 15,000 invited guests, Members of Parliament, foreign ambassadors and sundry aristocrats. Ironically, in view of the proposed name of the thoroughfare, Queen Victoria was in one of her reclusive moods following the death of her beloved Albert, so the task was deputed to the Prince of Wales and Princess Louise. The royal party was well protected by over a thousand policemen and members of the Grenadier and Coldstream Guards who were positioned along the official route.

After the loyal greeting by Sir John Thwaites and a speech from his Royal Highness, the inaugural cavalcade set off from Westminster to Blackfriars and then returned along the same route. This was the signal for temporary barricades to be removed so that the general public could at last enjoy a stroll along the carriageway. At least, such was the intention, but the genteel occasion was marred by what *The Times* referred to as 'a great mob of roughs' who were intent on celebrating in their own unique and somewhat inebriated style. Fortunately there were enough constables on hand to restrain the masses – *plus ça change!*

Public reaction to the new thoroughfare was generally favourable. Contemporary press reports extolled the virtues of the broad sweep of the embankment as a fitting addition to the treasures of the capital. However, nothing in this world is ever perfect, and criticism was directed at the mixture of architectural styles on display. For the purists the Victoria Embankment was something of a disappointment, and they regretted the lack of a uniform concept in the design of the buildings. Responsibility for these supposed aesthetic lapses can be laid at the door of no one individual. A more plausible explanation lies in the fact that artistic tastes changed during the construction work. It was precisely around 1870 that the Gothic Revival style began to wane – church inspired building forms gave way to what has been described as a Queen Anne style. Principal characteristics of public and commercial buildings adhering to this style included the use of brown and red brick plus the inclusion of Flemish inspired gables and dormers.

The celebrated architectural historian and connoisseur of Victorian London, Sir John Summerson (1904–1992), once commented on the 'miscellaneous' nature of the buildings lining the Embankment. He seemed impressed by the 'wonderfully diverse sizes, shapes and styles' to be found in this part of the capital. According to his notes, the range on the Victoria Embankment encompassed everything from English Perpendicular, French Renaissance and Jacobean to the 'modern Parisian' influence of the Hotel Cecil.

A more down-to-earth gripe from those citizens not particularly interested in architecture, who were used to taking a stroll beside the Thames, referred to the lack of shops and, more importantly on a hot summer's day, the complete absence of licensed premises, where a weary traveller could slake his thirst! Here the Victoria Embankment was a child of its age. Temperance and sobriety were the ruling virtues. Besides, a few hundred yards away along the Strand, just over fifty pubs, inns, alehouses and licensed restaurants existed to offer alcoholic libations. Therefore, so the argument ran, there was no need to sully the appearance of the Embankment with similar establishments.

It is worth remembering that Victoria Embankment was not the only jewel in the crown; plans were also well advanced for the Albert and Chelsea embankments. The foundation stone of the Albert Embankment was laid on 28th July 1866. The formal opening followed just over three years later, on 24th November 1869. The road, named after the Prince Consort, was constructed on the Surrey side at a cost of just over one million pounds. The carriageway linked Westminster Bridge with Vauxhall Bridge. Unfortunately, it was the only part of an 1862 scheme, suggested by Sir Joseph Bazalgette, to come to fruition. An embankment on the south side of the Thames from Westminster Bridge Road to London Bridge failed to materialise. Much opposition was encountered from wharf owners, and this caused the whole concept of a South Bank Embankment to be shelved indefinitely.

The Chelsea Embankment was more successful. The foundation stone was laid in August 1871, and the roadway was constructed above the low level intercepting sewer from Battersea Bridge to Chelsea Hospital. The inauguration took place on 9th July 1874.

This is an extract from Sir Christopher Wren's post-conflagration plan for the capital. The proposed forerunner of the present day Victoria Embankment is drawn on the map from the mouth of the Fleet River, westwards past the Temple Garden.

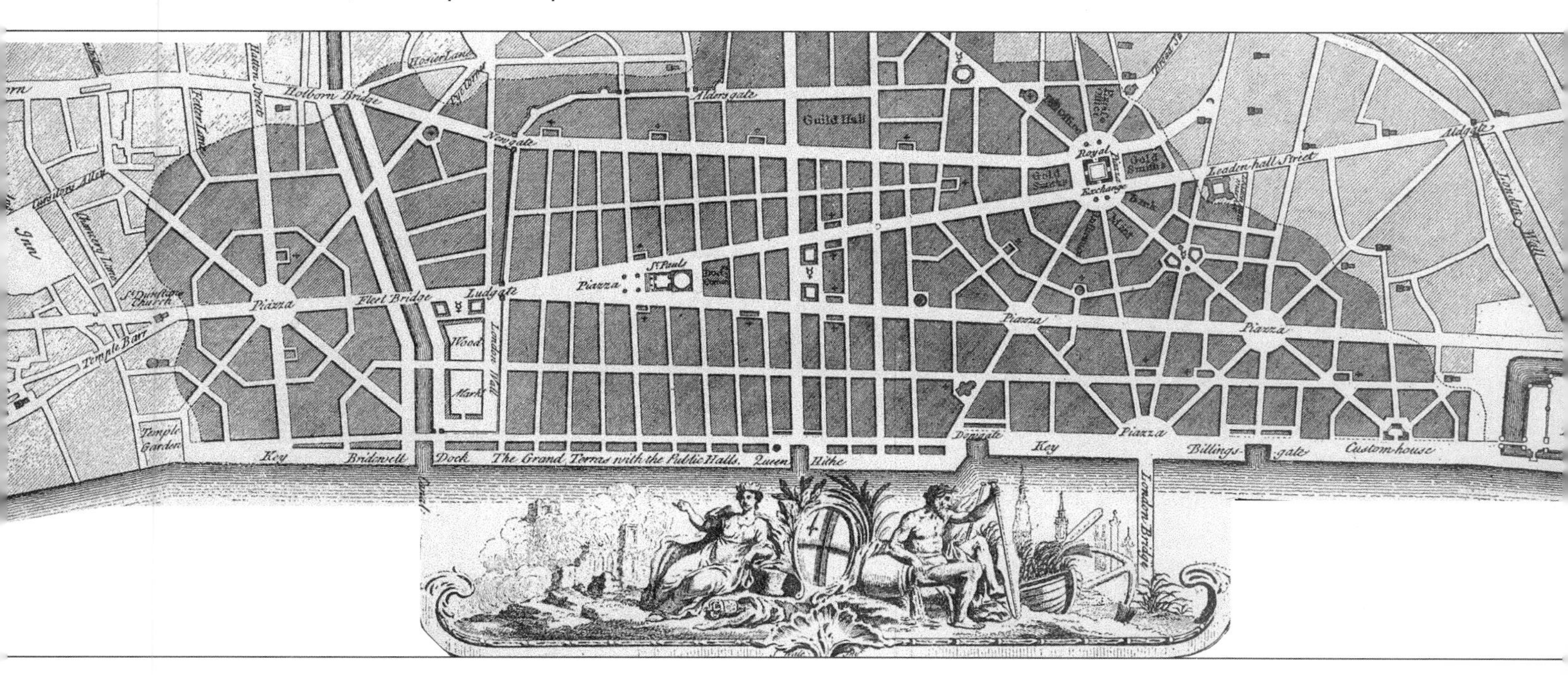

Chapter 2 ECHOES OF THE PAST

THE SIGHTS and sounds of today's Embankment are rooted in the past. Aside from the usual scenes of daily activity, the road has served throughout the years as a rallying point for marches or for lines of the politically disgruntled on their way to lobby Parliament. The broad avenue is ideal for accommodating ranks of protestors.

Crowds have also been attracted to the thoroughfare at times of national celebration. Then as now, each side of the carriageway is decked out in flags and bunting, the noise of the traffic is stilled and the grandeur of the occasion is enhanced. Coronation processions have passed this way in front of lines of cheering schoolchildren, gathered to salute the new monarch. Countless visitors to London have enjoyed strolling along the Embankment.

The broad sweep of the finished thoroughfare attracted many artists and photographers. An example is this engraving, executed in the summer of 1870, from the vantage point of Hungerford Bridge. In the distance is the familiar shape of the Houses of Parliament and Big Ben. The tract of land in the foreground by Whitehall Place was the subject of some 'rapacious designs' by the government, who wished to sell it for building development. Mainly through the intervention of W. H. Smith, MP for Westminster, the area was spared for 'gardens and public recreation'.

If we stand by the entrance to Westminster Bridge, at the southern end of the Embankment, the scene is dominated by Big Ben at the corner of the Houses of Parliament. The Clock Tower rises to a height of 320 feet (97.5 metres) and was completed in 1857. The hours are struck on the great bell of Big Ben – named after Sir Benjamin Hall (1802–1867), who oversaw much of the reconstruction of the Palace of Westminster and who was later appointed Chief Commissioner of Works. He was also an implacable opponent of street tramways in London, which were destined to play such a prominent role in the history of the thoroughfare where we are now. Across the road are the government offices in Portcullis House and the recently rebuilt Westminster station below it, both designed by Michael Hopkins and Partners.

Popular magazines and illustrated guides to London produced many views similar to this one, which householders of modest means could cut out and display in the sitting room. It features Waterloo Bridge and Cleopatra's Needle with a Thames paddle steamer approaching the camera.

Norman Shaw's New Scotland Yard, built in the 1880s, was the headquarters of the Metropolitan Police between 1890 and 1967. The building, on the west side of the Embankment, was described by A.P. Herbert as 'a very constabulary kind of castle'.

Just behind us are steps leading to Westminster Pier. Here, passengers can transfer to one of the many river steamers, which offer pleasure trips along the Thames. During the time of the 1951 festival, one of the most popular excursions was by the waterbus service, which operated from Westminster to the Festival Pleasure Gardens at Battersea. The present form of the pier came into being with the construction of the main body of the Victoria Embankment. It is a fairly utilitarian affair, but it has experienced a moment of comic glory, when in February 1955, its demolition and disappearance featured in an episode of the *Goon Show* on BBC Radio!

On the other side of the broad carriageway are the buildings that form New Scotland Yard. The former headquarters of the Metropolitan Police dates from 1891. The famous telephone number once associated with Scotland Yard – WHItehall 1212 – has figured in many popular detective stories and films.

The Boadicea Statue still stands guard opposite New Scotland Yard at the southern end of the Embankment – although, nowadays, the name of the legendary warrior queen has metamorphosed into Boudicca. Single-deck LCC tramcar 597 waits by the passenger shelter adjacent to the monument. This postcard view was sent on 9th May 1914, barely three months before the outbreak of the First World War.
J.B.Gent Collection

Glancing to our right, we view County Hall on the opposite bank of the river. This was for many years the headquarters of London local government, but is now used for other purposes. The large wheel structure of the London Eye is situated in the open ground next to County Hall.

We now pass Whitehall Stairs landing stage just before the road junction with Horse Guards Avenue. In the gardens between here and the entrance to Northumberland Avenue are several statues, the two most famous being those of William Tyndale, the translator of the New Testament into English, and of Samuel Plimsoll, the campaigner for seamen's rights and safety at sea. At the rear of the gardens on the landward side is Whitehall Court designed by Alfred Waterhouse in 1887.

Northumberland Avenue itself has a chequered history. The thoroughfare crosses the site of the former Northumberland House, once the London home of the Dukes of Northumberland. In the late 1860s and early 1870s much energy was expended in disputes over the proposed demolition of the property.

The junction of Victoria Embankment and Westminster Bridge from an upper storey window. The large building on the opposite bank of the Thames is County Hall, former seat of the London County Council. It was designed by Sir Ralph Knott, and the first section was opened by King George V in 1922. Nearer to the camera, we can note the sparse traffic on Westminster Bridge. On the left, an LCC tram, on service 56, is outbound for Peckham Rye and the Dulwich Hills.

The Royal Air Force Memorial dates from 1923 and was erected in memory of the 'officers and men of the air forces of the Empire, who lost their lives in the Great War, 1914–1918'. It is situated some 1,100 feet downstream from the junction of the Embankment and Bridge Street.

Eventually the matter of compensation was settled and the road was opened in 1876, but the public purse had been overstretched, and therefore, an opportunity was missed to develop the area into a truly fine avenue with buildings to match.

We arrive at Charing Cross Railway Bridge, commonly referred to as Hungerford Bridge, after the Hungerford Market that once existed here. We now pass under the tracks leading to Charing Cross Station, we note Charing Cross Pier, and on the opposite side of the road, Embankment Underground station – served by trains on the District, Circle, Bakerloo and Northern lines. The entrance to the station seems to be a popular place for flower sellers and newspaper vendors.

Beyond the Underground station lie Victoria Embankment

This animated scene dates back to around 1907, just after the trams started running along the Embankment. The rest of the traffic is all horse drawn and contains a large number of cabs. Some cabbies seem to be uncertain whether to stay in the main carriageway or to take advantage of the better paved tram tracks. The imposing building in the background, where Shell Mex House now stands, is the Hotel Cecil.

This mid-1930s colour view is included for its rarity value. Shell Mex House and the Savoy Hotel feature behind the trees. The partly visible building on the extreme left is Hungerford House, a former generating station for street lighting.

Gardens. This is a pleasant spot for relaxation in the summer, where Londoners can buy refreshments or just sit and contemplate a pleasant patch of green in the urban environment. Listening to music performed by visiting bands in the bandstand near the Villiers Street entrance has been popular since the opening of the Embankment. On the lighter side, the gardens have played host to many concerts over the years. *Open Air London*, published in 1939, had this to say: *All gardens have good displays of flowers, especially the Villiers Street division, which has an open air café. A band plays in the summer and the gardens then have a Continental air.*

A few years earlier, a correspondent of the BRITISH BANDSMAN, for 2nd September 1933, praised the staying power of the musical ensemble in residence: *The Hanwell Band were in excellent form last Sunday in the Victoria Embankment Gardens. During the Berlioz Selection, the bandstand lights went out, but the band continued to play notwithstanding. The lights were ultimately rectified . . .*

The fact that the instrumentalists continued, undaunted by their inability to make out the music in the gloom, was truly an example of the 'Dunkirk Spirit' – six and half years before the actual miracle evacuation took place.

An historical monument that predates the gardens is the York Water Gate, which once led to York House, erected in 1625 for the ill fated Duke of Buckingham. However, the size of the gate pales into insignificance against the backdrop of Shell Mex House and the Savoy Hotel. The former building, finished in 1933, was constructed on the site of the Hotel Cecil, which was opened in January 1896. Its competitor, the Savoy, started receiving guests from October 1889, and the whole hotel was renovated and enlarged in 1904. Needless to say, opinions were divided as to the merits of the 1930s' architectural styles hereabouts. Some folk found the massive stone tower of Shell Mex House, which reputedly contains the largest clock in London, somewhat overbearing. One wonders what they would have thought of the new Charing Cross Station.

Called by many visitors 'the two poshest hotels in town', only the Savoy was to remain after its next-door neighbour was pulled down in the 1930s. It was claimed in 1886 that the Cecil Hotel, on the left of the picture, was the largest of its kind in Europe. Guests had the choice of some 800 rooms!
J.B.Gent Collection

The building adjacent to Shell Mex House is the Adelphi. This rose in 1936 on the ruins of Adelphi Terrace, a celebrated row of houses constructed by the brothers Adam in 1768–1770. So the story goes, the brothers almost bankrupted themselves with this property development. However, the location later acquired fame as the home of several notables including the actor David Garrick, and the authors Thomas Hardy and George Bernard Shaw.

A structure of greater antiquity than the Adelphi is Cleopatra's Needle, which we observe on our right just before we come to Waterloo Pier. The obelisk was given to the nation in 1819 by Mehemet Ali, Viceroy of Egypt, but had to wait until 1878 to be put in place on the Embankment. The cost was underwritten by Sir William James Erasmus Wilson, and it is due to this worthy Victorian that the monument was finally extracted from the sands of Alexandria and shipped to London. Unfortunately the mystique of the pink granite object has been tarnished somewhat by the revelation that the Temptress of the Nile never had anything to do with it. In fact, the obelisk, which is one of a pair – the other resides in Central Park, New York – dates to the reign of the Pharoah Tuthmosis III and was orginally erected at Heliopolis about the year 1500 BC.

Cleopatra's Needle might be said to have led a charmed life. After being encased in an iron cylinder for the sea voyage from Egypt, it was nearly lost in a storm in the Bay of Biscay. The tempest, which occurred on 14th October 1877, claimed the lives of six seamen who were in charge of the floating pontoon. Landfall was finally made at Gravesend on 21st January 1878.

Its luck held out again on 4th September 1917, when eleven German Gotha type bombers launched an air raid on the capital city. A favourite strategy of the invaders was to follow the course of the Thames from the east coast until they could unload their deadly cargo. The attack resulted in 152 fatalities and also caused damage to Cleopatra's Needle when a bomb detonated in the roadway on the Embankment. Shrapnel tore into the pedestal and scarred one side of the obelisk.

Sightseers were quickly on the scene and the location acquired the status of an unofficial memorial to the first air raid on London. In 1919 the London County Council recognised this fact and decided not to repair the wartime damage.

Also damaged in the German attack were the two bronze sphinxes at the foot of Cleopatra's Needle. They were designed by G.J. Vulliamy, and were added as an afterthought; they were definitely not unearthed with the obelisk. Vulliamy's instructions as to their position on the Embankment were ignored or misinterpreted by contractors, with the result that they are now facing in the opposite directions to the ones the architect intended.

Our glance now returns to ground level as we approach the imposing structure of Sir Giles Gilbert Scott's Waterloo Bridge, completed in 1939, but not officially opened until 1945 (see chapter 8). One of the graceful arches of the bridge frames the scene in front of us, as we look at the former southern entrance to the Kingsway Subway. This tram tunnel once allowed passengers to travel onwards to north London. It closed in April 1952.

After we emerge from the shadow of the bridge, we are greeted on our left by the splendid façade of Somerset House. Construction of the present building commenced in 1776 and the work took until 1801 to complete. It was said that the central arch facing the river was placed so that the royal barge could enter directly from the Thames. For many years, visitors

The police constable in this late Edwardian picture of Cleopatra's Needle seems to be enjoying a gentle stroll in the spring sunshine. Was this a golden age, before the motor car laid claim to every square foot of road space? Note the passing tramcar and the elegant lamps lining this section of the Embankment.

Artistic views featuring the Embankment at night in the wet were popular in the 1920s and 1930s. The romantic nature of this scene is tempered by the fact that a number of unfortunates had to sleep out in conditions like these.

arriving by tram or taxi could pay their shilling to inspect family wills held in the probate section of the general register office. Government departments and the Inland Revenue once occupied most of the building; King's College, now part of London University, uses the east wing.

Waterloo Pier, directly in front of Somerset House, is one of the homes of the River Police. The service offered by the Metropolitan Police's Thames Division is much appreciated by those who make their living on the river. The job has its drawbacks and the task of pulling out suicide victims and sundry other flotsam and jetsam is not one of the most appealing aspects. As we look at the police station on the pier, we recall that the duty officer and his family once lived there, and that, nowadays, the regular 'beat' stretches from Tower Bridge to Richmond.

We pause opposite Temple Station, and then make for a nearby seat on the pavement adjoining the river wall. Temple Pier is a landing stage and is situated directly on the boundary between the cities of London and Westminster. Here we can sit down and observe the groups of joggers who pass at regular intervals – they seem to be out in all weathers. At least, the young people of today are not obliged to share the fate of the 'mudlarks' of the nineteenth century. In Victorian times, homeless scavengers would descend on the Embankment and then hang around the barges moored at the Thames piers in the hope of 'lightening the load' and selling what little they could steal in order to survive.

Now is a suitable moment to contemplate the vista, as we look along the line of the river, and to read what others have had to say about the scene in front of us. Gustave Doré and Blanchard Jerrold, writing in 1872, were obviously impressed by their new vantage point:

> *. . . between new Blackfriars Bridge and the railway bridge that is thrown alongside it, composing a curious scene of river, railway, and roadway traffic, crossing and passing in every direction, the river broadens and bends away on a bold southerly dip past the Houses of Parliament to Vauxhall . . . The greenery of the Temple, the noble lines of Somerset House, are a relief to the eye. Spires to the right and the left indicate the stretches of the great city through the heart of which the river flows.*
>
> *The Embankment changes the whole aspect of the scene as we pass under Waterloo Bridge . . . the great buildings are now piled on all sides. On the Surrey bank the Shot Tower and the Lion Brewery give a new dignity to the shore which is not yet embanked.*
>
> *The Adelphi buildings, the pointed roofs of the Charing Cross Hotel; the vastness of the brick railway station; the fine threads of the line carried across the river reach – with*

Tourists were (and still are) drawn to the Embankment with its decidedly varied collection of stone monuments, such as the Sphinx, seen here with Waterloo Bridge in the background. One wonders if this was a case of 'two's company, three's a crowd'?

Below left **This pavement artist is exhibiting his wares, hoping no doubt that the rain will hold off for a bit longer.**

glimpses of the new Westminster Bridge beyond . . . with barges and boats for foreground, that gives a gracious and lively idea of London on the Thames . . .

We also remember that the grandeur of the architecture is but one side of coin – the other is the poverty that is never far away. It is a sad fact that the bench we are sitting on may well offer a bed for the night for someone down on his luck. This was the fate of the Gloucestershire writer and composer Ivor Gurney (1890–1937), who actually slept regularly on the Embankment. This was more out of necessity than in response to an artistic desire to imbibe the ambiance of the place.

George Orwell described the Embankment tramps in *Down and Out in Paris and London*, published in 1933, and the author Thomas Holmes sums up the situation in *London's Underworld*:

Yes, on the Thames Embankment extremes meet, the ages are bridged, for the products of our up-to-date civilisation stand side by side with the products of primeval habits and nomadic life.

It is worth remembering that D. H. Lawrence depicted the area in both poetry and prose. Jack London and G. K. Chesterton – to name but two – have also contributed to the impression that a true reflection of the capital's poverty could be seen at night on the Embankment, with homeless human beings desperately huddled next to the Thames wall or in the lee of the bridges.

This stark assessment of the inequalities of modern life rather clouds our judgement, when we consider the wealth of the City of London. However, it has to be acknowledged that

Temple Gardens provide the proverbial oasis of peace in a populous city. Unfortunately, as this recent view demonstrates, access for the general public is very restricted. Entry to nearby roads is also barred by strategically placed concrete blocks. Twenty-first century security concerns have resulted in the ordinary citizen's freedom of movement being curtailed.

Victoria Embankment Gardens in early February – the crocuses are out. At lunchtime this is a favourite location where office workers can relax and take a break from their usual deskbound routine.

the City has also produced great benefactors, such as John Carpenter, whose financial bequest in 1442 led to the foundation of the City of London School, seen next to the street which bears the founder's name.

Our final port of call before crossing the threshold of Blackfriars Bridge is Unilever House – finished in 1932. This imposing building was designed by James Lomax-Simpson (1882–1976), and it features a number of impressive stone sculptures. One of these, depicting a horse with a girl, is the work of Sir William Reid Dick (1879–1961), who was also responsible for the sculpted eagle atop the RAF Memorial illustrated on page 26.

The Art Deco exterior of Unilever House was extensively renovated in 1980. At the same time, the opportunity was taken to collect and display some 500 works of contemporary British art. These now adorn the conference rooms and line the corridors and stairways of the building. Unilever House stands on the site of the former de Keyser's Royal Hotel. This luxurious accommodation was opened on 5th September 1874 by Sir Polydore de Keyser – a latter day Dick Whittington, who arrived as an immigrant from Belgium and worked his way up to become Lord Mayor. Before its demolition, the hotel that once boasted 400 rooms was used as offices for the Royal Flying Corps during the First World War.

This vista of the Thames, looking west from Blackfriars Bridge, reveals barges moored off the South Bank. On dry land, the motorman of a solitary LCC tram eases his charge around the curves leading to the passenger shelter on Victoria Embankment. People in those days could still saunter across the road without risking life and limb.

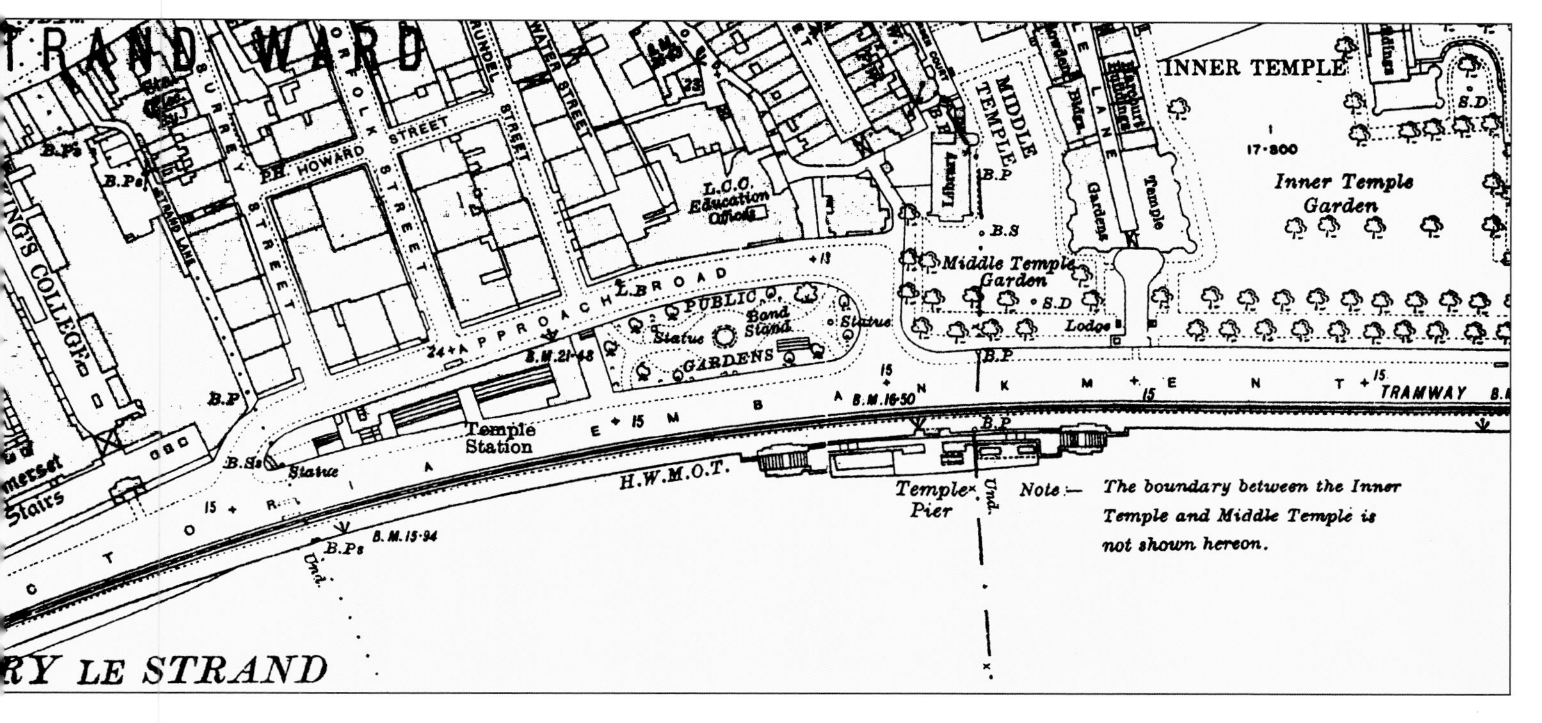

The Inner Temple and Middle Temple gardens and Temple Station feature in this extract from the 1916 edition of the Ordnance Survey 1:2500 map.

Blackfriars Bridge offers an excellent vantage point to view the buildings on the South Bank. Sea Containers House, Gabriels Wharf, the OXO Tower, the London Television Centre and the National Theatre are all grouped together in the space between Blackfriars and Waterloo bridges.

This detailed architectural sketch of the proposed de Keyser's Royal Hotel depicts an animated scene at the foot of Blackfriars Bridge. Note the contrast between the pleasure boat in the foreground and the work-a-day world of bargees. The inclusion of the horse bus on Victoria Embankment is probably a fanciful gesture, because it is unlikely that these vehicles were ever to be seen on a regular basis at this location.

On the next few pages we look in detail at some of the attractive features of the Victoria Embankment. Guarding Cleopatra's Needle is one of G.J. Vulliamy's inscrutable but imposing sphinxes. This seemingly exotic scene is tempered by the presence of London plane trees and a distinctive dolphin lamp.
All photos: James Whiting

Left **The fine detail of the base of one of C.H. Mabey's Dolphin Lamps, which line the banks of the Thames.**

Below **One side of the base with the date 1870 and a face which may represent Old Father Thames.**

The Lion's Head mooring rings which line the Embankment were designed by the sculptor Gilbert Bays. Even in Victorian times, one suspects that they were regarded more as an ornament rather than a practical way of securing the ropes of river craft. They can also be found on the opposite bank of the Thames adjoining the Albert Embankment.

For many years the columns supporting the lighting across the main carriageway of the Embankment were painted in a drab unrelieved, silver-grey colour. Careful restoration has now revealed the golden dolphins and coat of arms of the City of London and the erstwhile London County Council. These face the Embankment on both sides of the road in the respective territories of the Cities of London and Westminster. An English rose decoration appears on the pavement side.

Left **Winged sphinxes support the seats situated in the City of Westminster territory. They were originally cast at the SLB Foundry in Sittingbourne, Kent. After decades of use and long exposure to the sometimes pernicious London weather, they are still maintained in excellent condition.**

Bottom left **The seats that face the river in the City of London section of the Victoria Embankment feature a reclining camel motif, thereby echoing the Egyptian theme of Cleopatra's Needle and the attendant sphinxes. The design is attributed to C.H. Mabey. For some reason, one of these has also been installed at the Westminster Bridge end.**

Facing page top **York Water Gate, which predates the Embankment by over 200 years, is sometimes referred to as Buckingham Gate after the Duke of Buckingham, for whom it was erected in 1625. The intention had been to incorporate the structure into the Victoria Embankment at a location in front of Whitehall Gardens. However, Sir Joseph Bazalgette was frustrated in his plans and the scheme was dropped. The gate remained at the rear of the newly created Embankment Gardens. It was noted in an LCC survey at the end of the nineteenth century as being in 'a decayed state', but as can be seen here, subsequent restoration efforts have been successful. The design is attributed to the architect, Sir Balthazar Gerbier (1591–1667), and the gate once stood on the banks of the Thames. It is now marooned some hundred yards from the edge of the modern river.**

Facing page bottom left **ENGINEER OF THE LONDON MAIN DRAINAGE SYSTEM AND OF THE EMBANKMENT – so reads the inscription below the bust of Sir Joseph Bazalgette. This memorial to Sir Joseph was to a design by G. Simonds and was erected by the side of the Thames in 1899. It is a fitting monument to the 'Father of the Victoria Embankment'.**

Facing page bottom right **The boundary stone 'guarding' the entrance to the City of London supports this suitably melodramatic dragon grasping the City shield. Opinions vary as to the artistic merits of this particular edifice. Some find it totally hideous and believe it strikes a jarring note. Suggestions for its future include removal and consignment to a theme park!**

FLVMINI · VINCVLA · POSVIT
JOSEPH BAZALGETTE CB

CITY
OF
LONDON

Chapter 3 ON THE WATER

THE *CHARLOTTE DUNDAS*, constructed at Grangemouth in 1802, was the first viable steamboat. But it was dogged by bad luck and attracted opposition from local watermen before it could make an impact and win over its detractors. This objection to new fangled ideas also spread down south to the capital, where crews and owners of oar and wind powered vessels combined to see off the threat posed by a Mr Laurence in 1814. This particular gentleman had imported a steamboat from Bristol and had had the temerity to run a trial on Old Father Thames!

In the following year it was reported that a Mr George Dodd had brought a steam powered vessel all the way from Glasgow, and had commenced pleasure cruises on the Thames.

By the time of the inauguration of the Embankment in 1870, the new form of motive power had proved itself and the piers constructed adjacent to the thoroughfare at Westminster and Charing Cross were ideal for passengers wishing to 'commute' to other riverside locations in the metropolitan area. For those travellers whose sights were set further afield and who were intent on a good day out, Clacton, Southend and Margate were in easy reach by paddle steamer.

Unfortunately, throughout the nineteenth and twentieth

The arrival of steam traction in the first half of the nineteenth century introduced many citizens to the novel practice of using the Thames in order to commute to work. Somerset House seems to rise majestically from the waters, while assorted river vessels parade past the building. A new fangled paddle steamer heads out of the picture. Note the crew member perched precariously on one of the paddle boxes!

Headed The Disaster to the Cricket on August 27, 1847, **this contemporary print conveys the depth of the tragedy, as stricken passengers were pulled from the river. What was left of the boat seems to have beached itself on the Thames mud. The background gives some idea of the rickety landing stages and buildings, which were later swept away by the construction of the Embankment.**

centuries these handy conveyances had always been cast somewhat in the role of Cinderella. Many commentators have unjustifiably overlooked their contribution to the metropolitan public transport scene. And it is true to say that the Thames has been distinctly underused in the search for a solution to the traffic congestion problems, which occur on a daily basis near to its banks.

Part of the prejudice against 'taking to the water' may be due to the Londoner's traditional aversion to anything but dry land – the phrase 'if the Almighty had wanted me to cross water, he'd have given me webbed feet' is part of the folk wisdom of the native species. There was also plenty of evidence, real and anecdotal, of the perils of falling into the Thames. Raw sewage and effluent rendered any stay in the water a highly unpleasant and unhealthy experience. Many people couldn't swim, and observers on either bank of the river could often watch watermen fishing out human bodies, for which they were paid a retrieval fee.

A more reasonable objection to the mass use of steamboats centred on safety factors in an industry that at one time, unlike the cab and omnibus proprietors, was not subject to any form of licensing regulation or inspection. These anxieties about using the river on a regular basis were also rooted in sensational newspaper accounts of two tragic accidents.

The Halfpenny Fare Steamers operated by the Dyer's Hall Company began running in 1846 from a wharf near London Bridge to the Adelphi Pier. On 27th August 1847, the boiler of the *Cricket* exploded, killing 17 and leaving 60 severely injured. According to one report, part of the boiler was flung some 100 feet in the air towards the Adelphi Pier, while other pieces of metal debris were hurled in the direction of Waterloo Bridge. Most of the fatalities occurred amongst those who were in the cabin at the time of the explosion. Survivors were picked up by rescue boats or were able to wade ashore through the Thames mud.

The second disaster happened on 3rd September 1878, when a pleasure steamer, the *Princess Alice*, bound for Sheerness, sank in a collision off North Woolwich. Seven hundred out of the nine hundred passengers on board perished. This catastrophe effectively dented public confidence in river travel and can be said to have put paid to any further schemes of large scale investment in steamboats to rival London's local railways.

However, in spite of the bad press and public apprehension, the area where the Embankment now stands saw much activity in the heyday of the paddle steamer. It is estimated that, in the period from 1820 to 1824, around a million passengers a year were being carried. Of course, the element of risk added spice to even the shortest journey. Potential passengers were informed and cajoled by barkers employed by competing companies. For those unfortunates who didn't have their wits about them, the whole steamboat experience could be a traumatic one. It was often the case that the ultimate destination of the boat was decided by a majority vote of the travellers on board. People who didn't speak up for themselves could easily be inconvenienced by being taken in the wrong direction. They then risked being deposited on a Thames pier some way from their intended goal.

The Hungerford Market Steam Pier was a centre of steamboat activity as competing companies touted for trade on the river. Daily services by 'the fast and favourite packets *Sons Of The Thames* or *Princess Royal*' went from the pier to London Bridge and onwards to Southend, Sheerness and Chatham. Other boats included the General Steam Navigation Company's *Eclipse*, which left Hungerford Market Pier every weekday at 7.30am for Herne Bay and Margate. Those partaking of the voyage were offered an 'excellent plain breakfast at one shilling each', which could be consumed whilst listening to the on board band playing the latest tunes. According to the timetable, Margate was reached at 1.30pm, and after a quick turnaround the traveller could be back at Hungerford Pier by eight o'clock in the evening. Those poor souls who couldn't play truant for

This card was published by The Graphoscopic Co. of East Acton. From the restricted growth of the trees on the Embankment, this must be an 1870s scene at the rebuilt Westminster Pier. The lettering on the awning above the landing stage reads Greenwich & Woolwich Boats. Again, we notice that the paddlebox was a favourite vantage point for observing the river traffic. Umbrellas seem to be a popular fashion accoutrement – one suspects more out of necessity than a desire to be modish – cinders and smuts from the engine probably showered the passengers when the wind was in the wrong direction.

the day and who were tied to the run between home and office could avail themselves of frequent boats at thirty-minute intervals to slightly less bracing locations such as Blackwall, Greenwich and Woolwich.

At this point it is worth mentioning that the technology of paddle steamers enabled vessels to be very manoeuvrable when it came to docking at piers or moving 'crablike' from one bank of the Thames to the other. Paddle steamers also had shallower draughts than other more traditional river craft. This advantage enabled them to be used when water and tides were lower.

Although the Cammell-Laird shipyard in Birkenhead had produced the first screw driven ship, the *Robert F Stockton*, in 1838, this particular form of propulsion was always looked on as inferior to the traditional paddle wheel. It should also be added that many steamers operating on the river were double ended and thus could reverse smoothly with the minimum of fuss. For ease of operation under the Thames bridges, many boats possessed telescopic funnels and hinged masts.

As regards the art of navigation and its relevance to the steamboats departing and arriving at the Embankment piers, it

The *Thistle* was built in 1882 at Battersea for the London Steamboat Company and continued in service until 1908. She is depicted here at Waterloo Pier.
Guildhall Library

The Citizen Steamboat Company started in 1846, originally from Chelsea and Kew but later to piers below London Bridge. Their boats were iron built, painted black and had flush decks with below deck cabins fore and aft. They had tall black funnels with two red bands a little way down from the top which was bell mouthed with fancy top. They carried the City arms on the paddle boxes and on the inner or deck side of the boxes they were named after various City institutions e.g. 'Haberdasher', 'Fishmonger', 'Spectacle-maker', etc.
Guildhall Library

Boadicea **of the Thames Steamboat Company was a frequent visitor to the Thames piers. Here she is depicted just off the landing stage by Lambeth Palace. At least by the beginning of the twentieth century, some of the passengers were now protected from the elements by means of a canvas awning. This vessel continued in service until 1912.**
Tom Lee Collection

Below **This 1872–1879 edition Ordnance Survey map shows clearly Westminster Pier, the Underground station and Westminster Bridge.**

is useful to quote the following passage from the *1926 Royal Commission on Cross-River Traffic in London*:

At present there are 26 bridges across the Thames between the Tower Bridge and Teddington; all of these, with the exception of the Tower Bridge, are fixed bridges, and therefore have an important bearing on navigation.

Under existing circumstances, these bridges limit the size of all craft by the amount of headroom they allow, and by the fact that they prevent further dredging of the river bed. They also affect navigation by deflecting the normal current of the river, and retard movement by restricting visibility.

The navigator taking his vessel through the bridges has to think of at least four dimensions:–

The headroom of the arch, which varies with the rise and fall of the tide, coupled with the curvature of the arch.

The depth of the water under his keel, which also varies with the rise and fall of the tide.

The width of the arches to be negotiated, and the facilities which the springing of the arches give in this respect.

The length of the tunnel or passageway through the arch.

There are other factors, which have an important effect on navigation. The angle at which a bridge is placed between the river banks and its relation to the curvature of the channel are of great consequence, and particularly so in the case of Waterloo Bridge. Importance is also attached to navigation not being restricted to one, or even two, arches of a bridge, as a temporary obstruction of the navigation channel might compel the diversion of navigation to arches which were not previously intended or adequate for it.

This pre-First World War scene shows a paddle steamer heading for Charing Cross Pier, at the bottom left of the picture. The flags are flying above the Savoy and Cecil hotels, and on the carriageway below, a frequent service of trams shuttles its human cargo to all points of the metropolitan compass. J.B.Gent Collection

As an addendum to these words of wisdom, it needs to be stated that the 'rule of the road' on all waterways including the Thames is opposite to that traditionally applied to the Queen's Highway. All vessels must pass on the right. Near bridges and bends, boats going upstream must give way to craft proceeding downstream – and of course, steam should always give way to sail!

One of the Westminster landing stages was situated at the eastern end of Westminster Bridge, and in 1835 the London & Westminster Steamboat Company inaugurated a fleet of 'flower boats' – so called because they all bore the name of a flower inscribed on the paddlebox, which enclosed the eight feet diameter paddle wheel. Each vessel was rated at a top speed of 10.5 knots (19.5km/h).

Almost a century later, Westminster Pier (now transposed to the western end of the bridge) would experience an equally colourful visitor in the shape of steamer *Alexandra*. This was promoted as a showboat offering accommodation for 200 fare paying passengers, who could wine and dine the night away in the floating restaurant and cabaret. The cruise was to Richmond and back, but unfortunately this taste of the high life only lasted for one season in 1932. Bearing in mind the great depression was going on at the same time, perhaps the promoters were a little too over-optimistic in their venture!

Aside from the seasonal and pleasure traffic, there was only one serious attempt to establish a riverboat service which could be integrated with other parts of the capital's transport system. The pioneer was the London County Council – already the owner of a majority stake in the capital's tramway network. The transition from running vehicles on rails in the street to operating boats on the water highway serving the heart of the metropolis was meant to be a seamless one. In theory it was only a matter of time after the first thirty steamers were purchased until the service attracted enough passengers to make it profitable. In practice the whole experience turned out to be a dismal failure. Things started brightly enough with much pomp and circumstance surrounding the official opening by the Prince of Wales on 17th June 1905. The royal guest travelled from Westminster to Greenwich by boat and returned on a specially decorated tram to the (then) terminus on the Surrey side of

The inauguration of the LCC steamboat services attracted postcard publishers. The figure in the centre is the Prince of Wales, later King George V, and he is seen disembarking from the suitably regal sounding *King Alfred*. After the financial debacle, this vessel was sold to Glaser, Brewer & Co., and was later resold to serve as a steamer on the River Rhine in Germany.
Tom Lee Collection

The top deck passengers on LCC car 1371, which was heading for Tooting on route 2, have a good view of *HMS President*. This ship was once moored near the City boundary. She fulfilled the role of headquarters for the London Division of the Royal Navy Volunteer Reserve, one of whose members was the author's grandfather.
J.B.Gent Collection

This postcard view shows *BETA II*, moored by Hungerford Bridge. Her rather fearsome appearance is deceptive – what look like guns are in fact the nozzles of fire hoses. The three fire pumps could handle around 3,000 gallons of water per minute. She was built in 1906 at a cost of £10,600. She carried eight crew and was capable of a top speed of 12 knots.

Westminster Bridge. After the ceremonial inauguration the rest of the populus got the chance to sample the service, which ran from Greenwich to Westminster Pier, and from Westminster on as far as Hammersmith. All in all, some twenty-three piers were served. The fastest journey time between Westminster and Greenwich was 45 minutes.

The timetable called for a boat every quarter of an hour, with provision for a reduced fares 'workman special' at 6.30 in the morning, plus a number of express boats at peak periods. Return tickets were issued in conjunction with the tramways, thus giving passengers some flexibility, and return fares varied from tuppence ha'penny (1p) to sixpence (2.5p). Each vessel cost around £6,000 and measured 130 feet (39.6 metres) in length. One boiler supplied steam to diagonal compound engines which drove 10 feet 6 inches (3.2 metres) diameter paddle wheels. Maximum speed was calculated at 12.5 knots (23.2km/h).

Although the revenue figures for the summer seasons of 1905 and 1906 were reasonably respectable, chilly winter winds and bad weather affected takings from autumn to spring. According to reports reaching the LCC, the boats were difficult to handle, and the expertise with which some crews coped with Thames tides left much to be desired. The fact that the engines were too powerful was cited as a cause of a number of accidents.

The lack of passengers quickly became a cause for mirth. In the November 1905 edition of PUNCH, a cartoon, depicting dummy passengers being placed on an LCC steamboat, was headed:

A Suggestion To The LCC

Why not have artificial dummy passengers on the Thames steamboats during the winter months to replace the live ones who are not forthcoming? It would give quite a refreshing air of profit and popularity.

As an antidote to the pleasure steamers we observe the working life of a Thames Barge. The mast has been lowered to pass under Blackfriars Bridge. The river looks sluggish and this may be the reason for the chap, who is struggling manfully with a pair of oars at the bow of the boat. As usual, a cluster of passers-by has nothing better to do than to gawp at the antics of the boatmen. The date is around 1909.

On 1st November 1907, all the boats were moored in the Surrey Commercial Docks. Mounting losses had forced the closure and it was eventually calculated that the ratepayers would have to foot a bill for just under £140,000. The only benefit to accrue to the Council was the continued ownership of Greenwich Pier.

Thus ended the first 'modern' attempt to link the Embankment with other communities on the banks of the Thames. The idea was brought up several times in the 1920s and 1930s, but not even the powerful London Passenger Transport Board showed much interest in reviving the scheme. It was only during the Blitz that a serious effort was made to resurrect the service. In September 1940, the Port of London Authority supplied fifteen boats for the 'route' that linked North Woolwich with Westminster Pier. London Transport tram conductors were employed to check the fares, and vessels ran every half hour on weekdays and hourly on Sundays. Although none of the ersatz trams managed to get itself torpedoed by an enemy U-boat, mines and unexploded bombs did disrupt the schedule. This factor together with depressed takings caused the service to end definitively on 2nd November, just six weeks after it started.

After the Second World War, river craft continued to be used by the tourist and leisure market. For those 'would be sailors' who haven't yet found their sea legs, the tradition of keeping boats permanently moored next to the Embankment has been maintained, and the *Tattershall Castle* featured in the capital's club and pub guides. On this former Humber ferry paddle steamer, customers could party until the early hours.

The vessel underwent a major refurbishment in the winter of 2003–04, and was transported on a pontoon to a shipyard in Great Yarmouth. When she returns, she will rejoin another floating pub/restaurant, the Clyde turbine steamer *Queen Mary* – not to be confused with the Cunarder or with the brand new *Queen Mary 2*! She possesses twin funnels and was built in 1933 for excursion traffic out of Glasgow and along the River Clyde. She served as a troop carrier during the war.

Another former Clyde paddler, once moored at the Embankment, was the *Caledonia*. Unfortunately, she was severely damaged by fire in April 1980. Nothing could be done to restore the burnt out shell, and therefore, she was towed away to be broken up. However, her engines are now preserved at the Hollycombe Steam Museum in Hampshire, where they are occasionally steamed.

Scottish waters were also navigated by the *RS Hispaniola*, formerly the *Maid of Ashton*, built in 1953. She was moored at the Embankment in 1973, and now serves as an air-conditioned restaurant.

Another venue for social events and dinners is the *HQS Wellington*, which also acts as the Livery Hall of the Honourable Company of Master Mariners. Built at Devonport in 1934, the *Wellington* was sailed to the Embankment in December 1948, and underwent major refurbishment in 1991. The ship serves as a refreshment staging post during the annual procession of the Lord Mayor's Show. At this event a Thames barge is moored nearby so that a splendid display of fireworks can light up the City after dusk.

The ship located nearest Blackfriars Bridge is the *President*. This vessel was once *HMS Saxifrage* and saw service as a 'Q Ship' during the First World War. The Q type were disguised merchantmen, whose task was to lure German U boats to the surface for an attack. Covers were then thrown back to reveal guns which could open up on the enemy submarine. All this warlike activity is now firmly in the past, and the ship is now home to 'Interaction', an educational trust and charity.

Perhaps the most famous occupant of a berth next to the Embankment was *HMS Discovery*, which was launched in 1901 and made a vital contribution to Captain Scott's ill fated exploration of the Antarctic. The vessel was moored near Temple Underground Station in 1937 to serve as a training

We Help to Man the First Waterbuses of the War

(and make more Liquid History)

IT'S "Pass right down the boat, please," now. From September 13 London Transport has helped to man a regular Thames-steamboat service between Westminster Pier and Woolwich and carry thousands of passengers a day at 9d. return (7d. workman) for the full 10-mile trip of one or two hours.

At a few hours' notice landlubbing conductors of our buses and trams took to the deck like ducks to the water. They voted the ancient method of travel a nice change from spotting Request stops or calling "Mind the step." Instead they counselled "Hold your hats, ladies" in the bantering way of the Skylark man.

Some of them saw landmarks like Cherry Gardens or heard the name Brunswick for the first time. The old 'uns at their depots envied them their luck and recalled, wistfully, the last public experiment of a steamboat service, that of the L.C.C. from June, 1905, to October, 1907. Those 30 boats, all named after Londoners, had a stormy passage.

It has taken the greatest of wars to revive going-to-work by water. The event evoked a half-column leader in *The Times*, which voyaged buoyantly into Latin and then drifted to slang—"penny busters." And it added :

"It is safe to suspect that, of those who choose to go to work and back by the waterbus, very many will do it more or less for the fun of the thing. The voyage will probably not be so exciting as it could be one hundred years ago . . . in Woolwich Reach the Diamond steam vessel had tried to ram its rival, the Sons of the Thames."

Would A. P. Herbert Joke Again if—

Recalling the huge armament of words used in the "Boats-or-No-Boats Battle," *The Times* goes on :

"And yet, while welcoming the revival of the waterbus, its friends will watch its career with sympathetic anxiety. Suppose it were now, under these present conditions, to fail, would Mr. Herbert ever joke again ?"

[Mr. A. P. Herbert, M.P., affectionate friend of the Thames, began to champion the waterbus 10 years ago.] "No man has seen London till he has seen it from the river, as our fathers saw it," Mr. Herbert has written.

Yet a grey, rather than gay, London was what those first passengers of September 13, 1940, saw. But they were cheerful loads. "Hi, mate !" the Cockney bawled to a naval rating. "Ain't we got a destroyer to convoy us ?"

They were all pleasure steamers, these boats, with room for 180 to 250 people : their peace-time job was to take you to Hampton Court and such places. Several at least have done honourable service in the war : some dashed to Dunkirk, others have been hospital ship tenders. Now they relieve the streets : bus and tram tickets, as well as railway seasons, can be used.

Continued in previous column

"*Sure he* **did** *say garage, Bert* ?"

[*Beath*

From Thames to Trams

When the L.C.C. steamboats were sold, the fleet was scattered, some of it to the Swiss lakes, some even to the Tigris. Afterwards part of the staff worked in the L.C.C. Trams offices and even to-day there are some steering a pen in the greater family of London Transport.

The list is ever-shortening but to-day includes Messrs. J. C. Lowther and S. Barnes (Operation, Trams and Trolleybuses), W. G. Lawrence, R. Nicholls and F. Harris (Chief Engineers' Dept., Trams and Trolleybuses), J. Hutchings (Greenwich Generating Station), Vincent (timetables).

Pennyfare has just had a cheery note from another ex-steamboatman, Mr. M. H. Bates, who like Mr. N. Lawson retired from London Transport not long ago, and made a habit, almost a hobby, of keeping the liquid history of the L.C.C. To old friends he wishes good sailing, fair weather.

A.G.C.

This extract from a wartime edition of the London Transport staff magazine PENNYFARE gives a suitably upbeat account of the introduction of the waterbuses. Unfortunately, the optimism expressed in the piece was not justified, and the public would soon be saying a permanent 'Bon Voyage' to the vessels!

This is a modern day view of Westminster Pier with a City Cruises vessel moored, ready to receive passengers. Unfortunately, on this fine winter's morning there weren't many customers about! In the background is the RAF Memorial and Hungerford Bridge.
R.J. Harley

A bus crosses Waterloo Bridge, while below on the Thames the *Queen Mary* rests attached to a landing gantry. Although this involvement with the hospitality industry is one way of keeping vessels away from the scrap yard, opinions are divided among maritime enthusiasts as to the suitability of converting a ship into a floating pub/restaurant.
R.J. Harley

The *HQS Wellington* belongs to the Honourable Company of Master Mariners; therefore, it has a fitting place by the bank of the Thames alongside Victoria Embankment, within hailing distance of the City of London. The dolphins emblazoned on one of Bazalgette's splendid lamp columns add another nautical touch to the picture. R.J. Harley

The famous roundel used for London Underground and bus services has recently been adapted to show Transport for London's overseeing of river services. Capital Transport

facility and meeting place for the Scout movement. She managed to survive the war and was designated a RNVR Reserve Drill Ship at the time of the Festival of Britain. In 1954 she was reclaimed by the Admiralty, but was subsequently donated to the Maritime Trust in 1979. She finally left London for Dundee in 1986.

At the time of writing, London River Services, a division of Transport for London, has risen from the ashes of past failed attempts, and business at the Westminster and Embankment piers is now looking up. A commuter service links the Savoy Pier with Canary Wharf, whilst another operates between Chelsea Harbour and the Embankment. Leisure cruises depart regularly from Westminster in the direction of Richmond and Hampton Court, as well as serving the traditional tourist spots like Greenwich and the Tower of London.

People walking along the Embankment or waiting at one of the piers for a boat might care to ponder that in 2003 no fewer than 14,125 craft were licensed to use the River Thames – these included some 58 passenger steamers and 556 hire boats.

Chapter 4 Railways – Above and Below Ground

The lattice metal girders that form the main structure of Hungerford Bridge present the most visible evidence of the Victorian railway era at the Embankment. Since the opening of Charing Cross Station on 11th January 1864, many observers have castigated the bridge as an eyesore unworthy of inclusion in the grand vista from Westminster to the City. Perhaps some of the detractors were unaware of the published plans or were not moved to object when construction of the bridge commenced in 1860. Others may have been reassured when the prestigious name of Sir John Hawkshaw (1811–1891), an engineer of some renown, was linked to the project. Maybe the potential critics fondly imagined that the railway company would recreate the grace and style of the original Hungerford Suspension Bridge, opened in May 1845 to a design from the famous Isambard Kingdom Brunel.

Whatever the circumstances, the lattice metal girders have survived many concerted attempts to get rid of them; they have even resisted the bombing onslaught of the Blitz and the 'bridge nobody wants' has stubbornly stayed put until the present day.

The bridge linking the South Bank with Hungerford Market was regarded as an elegant addition to the sum of London river crossings. That it had such a short life-span was a disappointment to many. In this engraving, note the two hay barges nearest the artist. They were probably waiting their turn to unload at the pier by Hungerford Market. An ominous sign for the future of the bridge, which will later be sacrificed to provide railway access to the terminus at Charing Cross, is the presence of two steamboats in midstream.

It has been suggested that, if the politicians and planners had made the effort to consider the position of the new Charing Cross Station vis-à-vis the whole scheme of the Victoria Embankment, Parliament would never have granted permission to build the station and the connecting railway bridge across the Thames. As it was, there was always a suspicion that, having authorised the extension of the London, Brighton & South Coast Railway to Victoria, the elected members could not then refuse the South Eastern Railway its place in the sun on the Westminster bank of the river.

The original Brunel-inspired Hungerford Bridge was demolished to supply parts for the Clifton Suspension Bridge near Bristol. Only the redbrick piers sunk in the bed of the Thames were retained for use by the new railway bridge. Hungerford Market, situated at the Strand end of the bridge, suffered the same fate as Brunel's erstwhile cross river connection – although it is not recorded whether any pieces of its constituent structure were recycled into other buildings. As late as 1851, a large exhibition hall was added to the 1833 main building, but this last ditch attempt to make the place profitable failed to save the whole lot from being knocked down in August 1862 to make way for Charing Cross Station. It was reported

The entrance tracks to Charing Cross Station are depicted clearly on the 1872 map. Notice the cartographer's attention to detail in marking the position of every tree along the Embankment!

Victorian contemporaries of Charles Pooter, of *Diary of a Nobody* fame, would certainly recognise these last few yards of track leading from Hungerford Bridge to Charing Cross Station. R C Riley Collection

that the owners of Hungerford Market received the sum of £7,750 in compensation for their loss of trading premises.

Shareholders in the Hungerford Bridge did considerably better than their market brethren. Tolls from pedestrians brought in a steady revenue of around £25,000 per annum. The bridge originally cost £80,000 and was sold to the South Eastern Railway Company for a sum of £125,000.

On the Charing Cross Station site a large hotel was constructed facing the Strand. The building boasted some 300 rooms and was formally opened on 15th May 1865. A nice historical touch was added by the placing of a replica of the original Eleanor Cross in the station forecourt – the original had been smashed up in 1647 by some over zealous puritans! The Eleanor Cross was later used by the Ministry of Transport as a starting point from which all road distances are measured from central London to other parts of Britain.

If the French Renaissance style hotel and the Eleanor Cross were meant to impress the shareholders with the solid, reliable image of a new London terminus, then the railway company miscalculated when it came to the vaulted roof protecting the passengers from the elements. When it first went up, 'architectural aesthetes' pilloried the structure and, as if in response to the accusation of hideousness, the whole caboodle seemed to lose confidence in itself. The roof started to collapse on 5th December 1905, just as a gang of workmen were up aloft endeavouring to effect repairs. A mass evacuation of the

The modern Charing Cross Station complex and the new ascent to the Golden Jubilee Bridge form a background to the junction with Northumberland Avenue.
James Whiting

building was speedily put into operation and the crowds milling about on the Embankment could only watch in horror as the twisted frame of the glass and metal arched structure crashed through the station and demolished part of the nearby Avenue Theatre, which had opened in March 1882. It was said that the owner of the theatre received £30,000 in compensation from the railway company. Fatalities caused by the accident included two unfortunate workmen thrown from the roof. A bookstall assistant on the station platform and three pedestrians in the street below the station also succumbed when they were struck by falling debris.

Charing Cross Station reopened on 19th March 1906, and a replacement flat roof was constructed in the months after the disaster. This lasted some eighty years, until the demolition of the old station led to a radical new development arising in 1992. A nine storey office complex, designed by Terry Farrell and budgeted at £130 million, is now supported above the railway tracks by large columns. The area also features a shopping arcade and a new theatre 'underneath the arches'. The whole building has completely transformed the skyline as observed from the Embankment and Hungerford Bridge.

The number of tracks leading to the station has expanded over the years to cater for the increase in commuter trains. Hungerford Railway Bridge began life with four separate tracks, but in 1884 the approach to the station was augmented by three extra lines. This resulted in the footway on the south side of the bridge being sacrificed. Fortunately for those wanting to cross the Thames on foot, the north side of the bridge retained its walkway. People nowadays are not encumbered by the payment of a halfpenny toll to get from the South Bank to the Embankment. The railway company received almost £100,000 in compensation from the Metropolitan Board of Works after the passing of the Metropolis Toll Bridges Act in 1877 abolished these charges.

The layout leading to the station remained substantially unaltered until 1925/26, when much of the infrastructure was modernised in advance of the electrification of train services by the recently formed Southern Railway. On 28th February 1926, the new electric trains began to operate from Charing Cross to Orpington, Addiscombe, Hayes (Kent), Grove Park and Bromley North. A grand total of 88 track miles (141km) was brought into use. On that day in February 1926, it can truly be said that Charing Cross assumed the mantle which it has worn until the present time – that of a hectic commuter station served by electric traction.

The bridge was damaged by bombing during the Second World War. Extensive repairs were subsequently carried out in 1948, but it was only recently in 1979, that the wrought iron work supporting the original 1860s structure was renovated. This was but a preliminary to the complete 'makeover' which has transformed the structure at the start of the twenty-first century. Two futuristic looking footbridges, the Golden Jubilee bridges, now mask the original railway bridge, and they go some way to making this particular river crossing more attractive.

One of the original functions of the railway tracks was to carry shuttle trains from Charing Cross to Cannon Street. This round-the-houses jaunt was necessitated by the lack of a direct rail service between the West End and the City. The solution to this time-consuming detour lay in the construction of an underground railway that, quite literally, was woven into the fabric of the Victoria Embankment.

Construction methods employed on the pioneer 1863 Metropolitan Railway from Paddington to Farringdon favoured the 'cut and cover' approach, whereby wholesale excavation of the streets caused disruption to traffic and commerce. Into the resulting 'hole in the ground' a double track railway was placed. The road surface was then reinstated as part of the tunnel roof above the railway. Needless to say, this wholly inconvenient *modus operandi* found few advocates when it came to digging up main arteries of the capital such as Whitehall, the Strand and

The Golden Jubilee footbridges have completely altered the former, shabby looking structure of Hungerford Bridge. Only time will tell whether their presence will be enough to stifle the critics of the original rail bridge.
R.J. Harley

The crossing from Embankment Station over to the South Bank is now a pleasanter experience than it used to be with the old cramped footbridge right next to the entrance tracks to Charing Cross. Now, pedestrians have plenty of space and time to admire the river views. R.J. Harley

Fleet Street. The logical alternative was to route the trains via the new thoroughfare taking shape on the banks of the river.

The first section of the future District Line (then known as the Metropolitan District Railway) was inaugurated on Christmas Eve 1868, when steam hauled trains began to operate between South Kensington and Westminster Bridge stations. The latter was situated on the corner of Bridge Street and the Embankment. Charing Cross (Underground) Station was reached on 30th May 1870, where sidings were supplied to both east- and westbound tracks. This was the temporary terminus until a through service from West Brompton to Blackfriars commenced on 1st August of the same year. An intermediate stop called Temple Station was established between Somerset House and the City boundary. The end of the line at Mansion House was reached on 3rd July 1871.

Instead of walking the length of the Embankment, travellers desirous of commuting from Westminster to Blackfriars could now avail themselves of a frequent service of trains offering three classes of travel accommodation. Short, four-wheeled coaches were the norm, and the standard of comfort varied from the upholstered seats of the well-to-do first class to the hard wooden benches occupied by the unfortunate third class passengers. Those who wished to smoke on their journey were out of luck. In a gesture which now looks very farsighted, the cigarette, cigar and pipe brigade were thwarted by the management, who insisted on a complete ban. This was overturned in 1874, but was reintroduced as part of general health and safety laws in 1984.

It soon became obvious that soot encrusted tunnels, crowded carriages and steam locomotives made for a very messy way of travel, even in the plush first class compartments. All three stations situated on the Embankment were constructed in part at least so that air and light could penetrate from the outside. They were not totally enclosed like present day tube stations. However, this did not solve the problem. It should be mentioned that the use of the tunnels had increased after 6th October 1884, when the Circle Line opened. Originally, District trains ran anticlockwise and Metropolitan stock maintained the clockwise service, all of which added to the grime and dirt.

A contemporary newspaper report catches the mood, when it describes a delay in the tunnel between Temple and Blackfriars. The narrative centres on the gripes of many City gents, who arrived late at their places of work 'looking as if they had just emerged from a coal mine'. As regards several ladies on the train, their silks and satins were said to be ruined. In winter this state affairs must have obliged many folk to forsake the smut and grime of the District Railway trains for the smut and grime of a London 'peasouper' on the surface! Clearly the solution lay in a change of traction, which would put steam locomotives out to pasture.

The wonder of electricity transformed public transport in the late Victorian and early Edwardian eras. Amazing developments happening in North American soon filtered across the Atlantic, although it sometimes took several years for the conservative British to exploit the new technology. Thus it was that the tracks under the Embankment were energised for public service on 1st July 1905, and the Underground, as we know it today, began to assume a familiar aspect. By this time, anyone waiting on the platform at Westminster Station had the opportunity of reaching quite a few places on the Underground system.

At this point, before describing the advent of deep level underground railways, it is worth digressing to discuss a forerunner of the tube, which didn't quite make it to commercial operation. The Whitehall and Waterloo Pneumatic Railway Company was established in 1865 to construct a line from a station on the Embankment, near New Scotland Yard, to

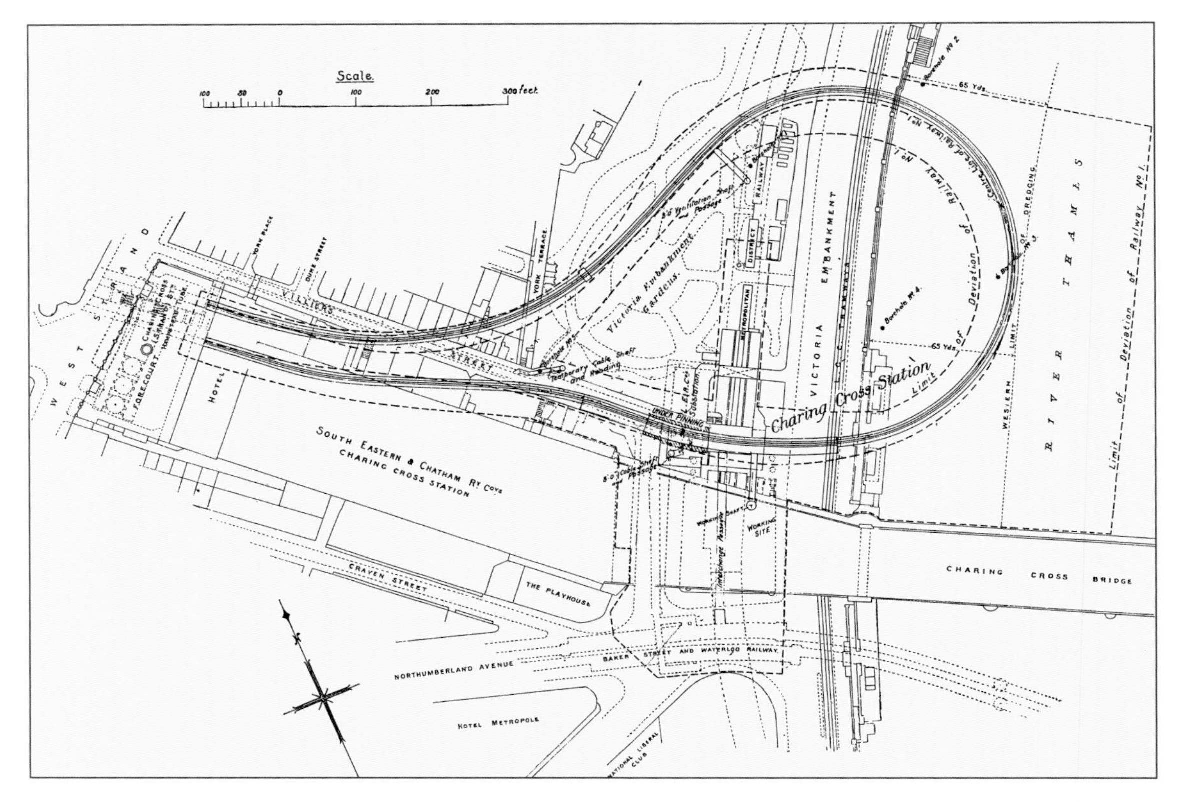

This diagram appeared in the TRAMWAY & RAILWAY WORLD for 11th December 1913. It shows the position of Charing Cross main line station with the proposed underground location for the terminal loop of the Hampstead tube line. Among all the details one can make out the District Line station, the tram track with a loading island just above the course of the Bakerloo Line, and the layout of Victoria Embankment Gardens and the local streets.

a terminus adjacent to Waterloo Station on the South Bank. The technology to be employed was based on the 'atmospheric railway' principle, which (worryingly for the investors) had already failed in mainline tests conducted between London and Croydon in 1845–46. Each carriage was attached to a piston, which fitted into a supposedly airtight pipe. The difference in air pressure, created by a pneumatic pumping station linked to the pipe, caused the piston to move the train – in theory, at least.

Financial crises delayed construction work and, in spite of the cheerful predictions of the promoters, neither trains nor the promised clean and frequent service materialised. The famous railway contractor, Thomas Brassey, finished the tunnel, but he had no further use for it and the whole structure was sealed off, thus bringing down the curtain on the Whitehall and Waterloo Railway.

The arrival of tube railways in London was a world first for the capital. The electrically powered City & South London Railway opened on 4th November 1890 and soon the place was awash with plans for new lines. Here, a note of caution is appropriate. There is something about human nature that makes 'get rich quick schemes' deceptively attractive. Investors in tube railway stock in the 1890s were akin to those who rushed to join the 'dot com' boom a century later. And the results were just as disappointing.

Tube promoters practised all sorts of financial hocus-pocus in order to inveigle cash out of the general public. There were casualties on every side. One gentleman, a certain Whitaker Wright, was convicted in 1904 of defrauding investors of some five million pounds. His Baker Street and Waterloo Railway Company was at the centre of the scandal. After being convicted and sentenced to seven years' imprisonment, the unfortunate Wright committed suicide by ingesting cyanide.

In spite of the coffers being distinctly lightweight, the Baker Street and Waterloo Railway, as authorised in an 1893 Act, opened on 10th March 1906. It had been rescued by another 'larger than life' character, the American traction magnate Charles Tyson Yerkes, who, in association with the banker Sir Edgar Speyer, had created the Underground Electric Railways of London Ltd.

Interchange facilities were constructed for passengers transferring to District trains at Charing Cross Station. Travellers descending from the Embankment had the choice of two terminal destinations, at Baker Street and Lambeth North respectively. Newspaper reporters soon conspired to shorten the name of the railway company with headlines promoting 'the Baker-Loo, London's Latest Twopenny Tube!' The name (without the hyphen) then stuck and the Bakerloo took its place in metropolitan transport mythology.

The Bakerloo was a contemporary of the Hampstead Tube (officially, the Charing Cross, Euston & Hampstead Railway), which opened on 22nd June 1907. To add to the confusion, its terminus was also known as Charing Cross, although the name was later changed to the Strand. Tracks were prolonged from the Strand to a loop terminus under Charing Cross Embankment Station in 1914. What was to become part of the future Northern Line was later extended under the Thames to Kennington, and the service was inaugurated on 13th September 1926.

The idea of placing an Underground station behind a classical façade was a novel one, and here at Temple the experiment paid off. The original station sign has been kept in pristine condition and, together with the familiar red telephone box, graces a scene which most Londoners would instantly recognise. Capital Transport

An interesting proposal was made at the time when the Hampstead Tube was contemplating an extension to the Embankment. The splendidly named 'Improvements Committee of the London County Council' came up with an idea for a pedestrian subway under the Thames. A figure of £5,000 was suggested as the cost of the project, which was outlined as follows:

There would be stairways on each side of the Embankment, and a direct communication also with the eastern platform of the Metropolitan District Railway Station, whence lifts would communicate also with the Baker Street and Waterloo, and Charing Cross and Hampstead railways.

Unfortunately, nothing came of this scheme, which would have offered a useful alternative to Hungerford Bridge, especially in bad weather. Work began in the 1920s to extend and modernise Charing Cross Underground Station. Let the TRAMWAY & RAILWAY WORLD of 14th March 1929 take up the story:

Work began in 1926. A new circulating area was first constructed beneath the District Railway tracks at a point where passengers could conveniently change between that railway and the Bakerloo and Hampstead tubes below . . . two new escalators were then constructed to link up the intermediate hall with the new southbound platform of the Hampstead tube. These are of the cleat comb type similar to those recently installed elsewhere on the Underground system.

The next stage in the scheme was the installation of two escalators which run from the street level (Villiers Street) to the intermediate landing. These were opened for traffic on 4th December 1928, and were the first escalators to be installed at a District Railway station. The four escalators added during the reconstruction bring the number at this station to eight. Their value in speeding the transit of passengers from the street to the train is indicated by the fact that the journey from the District platforms to the street level, which formerly took 60 seconds, now takes only 30 seconds. There are no fixed stairways to cause delay through congestion.

Finally, the narrow arcade booking office connecting Villiers Street with the Embankment was cleared away and a new hall, three times as large as the old one, was built. The hall extends practically the whole length of the District Railway platforms. It is 112ft long, 83ft wide and has an area of 10,000 square feet. It is 13ft high, with a centre clerestory of 18ft, and is supported on massive steel columns. These columns, which are encased with terracotta tiles, are entirely in keeping with the design of the hall. The floor is paved with durus tiles, similar to those used at the new Piccadilly Circus Station. As at that station, automatic ticket machines are being installed at Charing Cross.

The mention of the booking hall brings to mind another side to the building that was meant to appeal to the higher instincts of the mass of weary commuters. The hall was often the venue for a number of exhibitions, which promoted British industries. The scope varied over the years from an assembly of ladies' evening wear designed by LCC art students to a gleefully 'over the top' model railway layout that caused major passenger congestion amongst small boys of all ages!

The following snippet appeared in the May 1932 edition of the Staff Magazine issued to employees of the Underground Group, which once controlled a large section of London's passenger transport network. The choice of exhibits is nothing if not eclectic . . .

From 31st March until 17th April an exhibition of British goods – glass, clocks, leather goods, metal fittings, pottery, electric light fittings, etc, etc, was held in the booking hall, Charing Cross Station. It was arranged by the Design and Industries Association, and the exhibits were chosen for their simple and efficient design from goods provided on a commercial scale and sold at moderate prices.

Charing Cross Underground station (today's Embankment station) for many years hosted small exhibitions in the ticket hall. This 1932 view shows one mounted to display household electrical appliances. LT Museum

The aim of the Design and Industries Association is to promote a good standard of design in the products of British industry, and the object of the exhibition was to show that mass production need not mean ugliness and poor workmanship. This beauty does not lie in faking material or added ornamentation, but in excellence of design, material and workmanship.

Visitors to the booking office hall have included such worthies as Lord Ashfield, Chairman of the Underground Group, and prominent London politician, Herbert Morrison. This tradition of mounting displays for the public continued well after the formation of the London Passenger Transport Board in 1933.

The saga of Underground railways at the Embankment can now be brought right up to date. The last chapter began in 1979, when Charing Cross Station was renamed Embankment Station, thus avoiding confusion over the status of Strand Station. This latter assumed the title of Charing Cross, when the Jubilee Line was opened on 1st June 1979. The most recent major alteration in services occurred on 22nd December 1999, when Westminster Station finally lost its unique District and Circle Line status and gained a genuine tube railway in the guise of Jubilee Line trains from Stanmore to Stratford.

Arrival by Jubilee Line train at the new Westminster Station evokes mixed emotions. The functional, but not unattractive, modernism of the station platforms is in stark contrast to the vast cavern that holds the escalators leading to the surface. The bare concrete pillars, which support the building above, and the nets draped to prevent roosting pigeons, create a depressing and soulless atmosphere. The impression is a long way from the harmonious designs pioneered by Messrs Holden and Pick in the 1930s!

Blackfriars District Railway Station was originally constructed directly under the four track London Chatham & Dover main line to Ludgate Hill Station. This view was taken on 24th August 1973, in the halcyon days before politicians and privatisation conspired to alter permanently the nation's transport system. The sign, British Rail Blackfriars, now invites a certain wistful nostalgia!
J.C.Gillham

Platform level at Blackfriars, on 9th August 1973, and we are looking west towards the tunnel leading under the Embankment. Note that part of the station is open to the elements – this was typical of many of the sub surface District and Metropolitan Line stations on the London Underground network, dating back to the days of steam locomotives.
J.C.Gillham

Chapter 5 ALWAYS A TRAM IN SIGHT

THE FIRST successful horse tramways in the metropolitan area started to operate in the 1870s. From then on it was always a struggle for tramway companies to obtain the necessary Parliamentary legislation to expand the system into the centre of town. There were just too many vested interests unwilling to let a form of transport, which wealthy influential people associated with the poorer working classes, pass by their front doors. All manner of arguments were advanced to keep the trams out, and of course, the omnibus proprietors were quite happy to steal a march on their railbound rivals. Buses could tap all the traffic in the cities of London and Westminster, while the trams were banished to the outlying streets. It should be mentioned here that trams offered lower fares than buses, and they were obliged to run special services for workmen and artisans.

In an ideal world the Victoria Embankment would have presented no problems for a horse tramway service. The thoroughfare was devoid of severe gradients and was certainly wide enough to accommodate double track. It had already been established in the Parliamentary session of 1872 that Whitehall, Trafalgar Square and the Strand were 'no go areas' for tramways, therefore, an alternative routeing via the Embankment might have seemed eminently sensible to any impartial observer. In practice, everyone who mattered in the decision making process had some sort of political axe to grind, and the resulting prejudice kept trams from using the Thames bridges. A 'cordon sanitaire' was maintained by Parliament so that the nearest tram rails got to the Embankment from the north side of the river was at termini in Grays Inn Road and at Aldersgate respectively. Because of the 1872 ban there was no immediate prospect of tracks approaching any closer to the northern banks of the Thames.

On the Surrey side of the river, tramlines first reached the eastern approach to Westminster Bridge in August 1861, but the service to Kennington lasted but a few months before the American promoter, George Francis Train, was obliged to admit defeat. A more durable horse tramway connection from Belvedere Road to the rest of the South London network opened on 23rd December 1870 and this survived until the inauguration of electric traction on 15th May 1903. However, the impasse of getting tramways across the Thames remained. The ban on the use of Westminster and Blackfriars bridges effectively blocked access to the Victoria Embankment.

The situation was summed up concisely by these words of wisdom, which appeared in the TRAMWAY & RAILWAY WORLD for 18th June 1904:

Parliament treats London as it treats no other municipality . . . the London County Council has appealed to Parliament for sanction for the Embankment tramway not less than three times. The bill is usually passed by either one of the two Houses, which with charming inconsistency rejects it the following session . . . No adequate reasons are ever presented against the bill. The stock argument is that the Embankment is a fine, wide thoroughfare, that it forms a pleasant drive, and that it would be a pity to spoil its amenities by constructing a tramway along it.

The working men who cross Westminster Bridge have, we imagine, scarcely the same power of choice. They must cross the bridge by tramway or they must walk. At present it is a case of Hobson's choice . . . The financial aspect of the Embankment tramway with a connection over Westminster Bridge is an important one. There can hardly be any doubt that it will prove highly remunerative, and the Council's tramways need whatever advantage can be obtained in this way.

One sentence in the last paragraph of this 1904 editorial shows remarkable prescience:

In time, doubtless, Parliament and the police will learn that the best remedy for streets congested with cabs and omnibuses is a modern tramway . . .

Just over a year later, the editor of the TRAMWAY & RAILWAY WORLD had moved on from pure criticism – he was now fairly incensed by the behaviour of certain members of the House of Lords in blocking yet another attempt by the LCC to get legislation passed:

The measure had passed the House of Commons after an amicable agreement had been arrived at – between the County Council and the City Corporation. Blackfriars Bridge was to be widened and the tramway made, and it was naturally supposed that the bill was safe. But the reactionaries in the House of Lords gathered all their forces, and when the bill came on there was a solid phalanx of these Peers in attendance prepared to die in the last ditch if necessary for "the preservation of the beauties of the Embankment" and to maintain that the tramway was not necessary.

In fact the attendance – it numbered nearly 100 – was greater than it is in many occasions when first class matters of state are under discussion, and after the unhappy bill had been killed, those patriotic Peers melted away . . . The Peers who voted against the bill showed that they represented no one but themselves, and nothing but their own selfish interests as the owners of carriages, horses and motor cars by their colossal ignorance as to the needs of London and the state of public opinion.

All of which leaves everybody in no doubt that the Lords' veto was based strictly on social class lines. But it is a tribute to the LCC and to the single minded doggedness of the members of

Many lantern slide views were used to illustrate new building projects in the capital. This construction scene depicts the new conduit tram tracks. Nearly all work was done manually without any mechanical aids.

LAYING THE L.C.C TRAMS
ON THE VICTORIA EMBANKMENT.

the Highways Committee in particular, that they eventually succeeded in overcoming the opposition. On 4th August 1906 the bill finally received the Royal Assent, and work started four weeks later on the new venture. The tender from Messrs Dick, Kerr & Co. at £45,836 14s 2d for 3.23 miles (5.2km) of single track was accepted by the Council.

It is important to remember that the London County Council system in central London used the conduit method of current collection, in which two T-shaped current rails were housed in a conduit between the running rails. This dispensed with overhead wires and thus found more favour with environmentalists, who wanted an uninterrupted view of the blue vault of heaven.

Preliminary works were necessary before tracks could be laid on the northern side of Westminster Bridge. These involved realigning the tramway junction at Westminster Bridge Road and Stangate, just outside St Thomas's Hospital. The opportunity was also taken to repave the roadway with wooden blocks instead of the conventional granite setts. This use of mainly Jarrah hardwood, imported from Australia, was sanctioned in an attempt to deaden the noise of passing road vehicles in front of the hospital.

The installation of double tram track on the bridge presented no extraordinary problems. It was noted at the time that LCC engineers and their hired contractors had already had experience of fitting the permanent way to Vauxhall Bridge, and they brought this knowledge to bear at Westminster. The sharp curve by the Boadicea Statue entailed the use of 'specially heavy check rails', and construction at this point resulted in the cutting down of one tree – the only such loss in the entire extension project.

As gangs of labourers settled along the Embankment, it became apparent that, in the years since the opening, the maintenance of the highway had been neglected. In short, road and pavement levels varied somewhat. A surveyor's report states that under Waterloo Bridge the northern footpath was found to be some three feet higher than the southern one! Many of the kerbstones had to be removed and reset; parts of the carriageway, not containing the tramway, had to be levelled and resurfaced, thus benefiting other road users. Indeed, so thorough were Messrs Dick, Kerr's workmen in digging new drains, that they unearthed some of the old timber piling, some of which must have dated back to the 1860s.

The most complicated piece of new trackwork was situated at

Left **In the 1920s the tramways were a well established feature of daily life on the Embankment. On a pleasant summer's day the only jarring note in this view at Blackfriars is the ugly looking passenger shelter. The structure, which for a short time played host to the LCC's 'tramophone' experiment (described overleaf) was eventually demolished in 1953.**

the entrance to the Kingsway Subway. Here a three way junction was installed, which necessitated a full reconstruction of the 'roof' covering the District Railway. Brick arches dating back to the opening of the railway had to be replaced by a raft of steel girders. In theory, all work had to be undertaken without interrupting the train service. It should be noted that a pointsman stationed on the river footpath originally worked all facing points. This speeded up the service by not requiring each motorman to descend from his tram and change the point blade manually by means of a point iron. Other pointsmen were employed at strategic intervals along the Embankment. Their most useful function was to assist tram crews should any difficulties occur at trailing crossovers. These reversal points were situated at New Scotland Yard, opposite Northumberland Avenue, either side of Waterloo Bridge – at Savoy Street and outside Somerset House. The temporary terminus to the line was by John Carpenter Street just short of the approach to Blackfriars Bridge.

The great day arrived on 15th December 1906, when trams began carrying the general public. Passengers waiting at the Blackfriars end of the Embankment had a choice of tramcars linking John Carpenter Street to Battersea Park Road, Tooting, Streatham and Dulwich. A short walk down to Savoy Street brought the traveller to the terminus of further services to places such as Tower Bridge, Blackwall Tunnel via Greenwich, and Greenwich via Peckham.

The main tramway feature along the Embankment was the southern portal of the Kingsway Subway. This underground tramway, which burrowed under the heart of the capital, was a unique achievement. In the shadow of the earlier Waterloo Bridge, a single deck tram emerges into the sunshine. An illuminated sign BEWARE CARS CROSSING plus a policeman and several tram inspectors should minimise the danger of collisions at this junction. J.B.Gent Collection

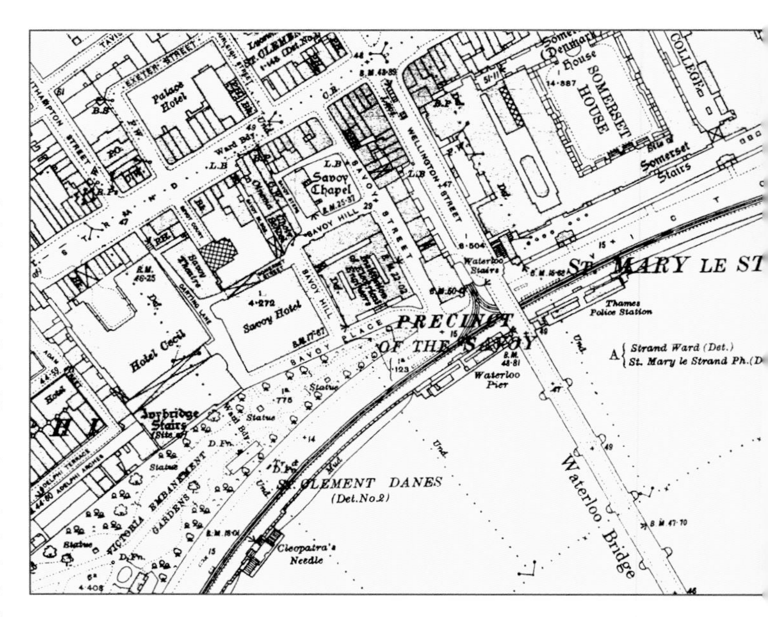

The triangular tramway junction at the entrance to the Kingsway Subway is shown on this 1916 Ordnance Survey map.

All went well, with only a few teething troubles reported in the first months. The only criticism expressed by potential passengers was the 'inconvenience' of having to cross the whole carriageway from the 'Strand side' to reach the tram tracks by the river footpath. It seems that, even in 1906, people crossing the road had to be nimble in order to avoid the stream of cabs, horse drawn vans, steam lorries and the odd private motorist in his automobile.

The tramway status quo did not remain for long. On 10th April 1908, the Kingsway Subway became operational, thus providing Londoners with an excellent cross-capital transport facility. Single-deck cars emerged from the shadow of Waterloo Bridge to join their sister vehicles on the Embankment. The original subway services were from Highbury Station to Kennington or Tower Bridge. Only the southern curves leading from the subway portal were used initially. The eastern set only saw a restricted service in 1909, after connecting tracks on Blackfriars Bridge were opened on 14th September. Thereafter, they were little used and were removed entirely in 1930.

On the opening up of Blackfriars Bridge for tramway traffic, it became possible for trams running from south London suburban termini to make a loop via the Embankment. Paired routes reflected this arrangement. Thus, for example, a route 36 car on the journey from Abbey Wood would normally proceed via Blackfriars Bridge and return across the Thames by way of Westminster Bridge. Route 38 trams ran in the opposite direction. However, some routes not partaking in the 'Embankment Circles' continued to terminate at Savoy Street and at John Carpenter Street.

For those, who for the purposes of work or enjoyment, needed transport in the wee small hours, the following extract from Round & About London by Tram gives the relevant information:

When London sleeps, the LCC cars on nine routes are still threading the quiet streets for the benefit of thousands of workers who toil at night. They begin to run from Victoria Embankment about 12.30am and repeat the journeys at intervals until about 5am, when the day cars continue the 'services that never cease'. The all night cars run to Lewisham and Catford, Brixton, Tooting Broadway and Battersea in the south . . .

When it was cold and dark, a refuge from the elements could be found in one of the passenger shelters installed at either end of the Embankment. In the one situated near John Carpenter Street the LCC conducted a rather novel experiment. The Tramway & Railway World of 4th May 1911 enlightens readers:

A telephonic indicator, which is the patent of Messrs Alfred Graham and Company, and which has been termed a "tramophone", is being given a trial in the western half of the shelter. This is the first occasion that it has been introduced in England, and if it proves successful the installation will be extended. It is an ingenious combination of the short distance telephone and the phonograph, so that the voice of the regulator stationed at a hall 200 yards further along the Embankment can be heard by the officials regulating the queues and the people at the head.

The moment a car for any one of the south London routes to be reached from Blackfriars Bridge passes this further point, a message, telling its destination and the accommodation inside and out for passengers, is telephoned through and heard by the people at the head of the waiting lines.

The first trial of the device took place on 21st April, at the commencement of the period of the evening pressure.

"Clapham car coming up," buzzed a strange voice.

"Room for 12 inside and four out."

The waiting passengers pressed closer together and looked all ways at once to discover whence the sounds came. They saw then what they took to be the horn of an inverted gramophone hanging above their heads when their car arrived, and the Tooting passengers in the next corridor were told that their car was on the way with vacant seats for 15 inside and 20 out.

Thus, the first stirrings of the 'information era' hit the airwaves. Subsequent generations of travellers at stations, bus stops and airports can trace the surfeit of information (or lack of it!) to a lone pioneer barking out instructions by the banks of the Thames – he even had time to mention how many spare seats were to be had on the next arrival. It is a pity that no one in authority has yet found the time to erect a blue plaque to record this historic event.

During the First World War the trams acquitted themselves well when it came to transporting numbers of extra workers employed in the City and at Government offices. Almost a year after the conflict ceased, a national railway strike, which lasted

The Kingsway Subway was reconstructed in 1930-31 to take double deck trams. Further civil engineering work was necessary when Waterloo Bridge was replaced in the late 1930s. A tram on route 31, from Hackney to Wandsworth, waits for the all clear to cross the road, whilst all around, John Rennie's masterpiece is being dismantled.

New trackwork, depicted here, was required for the rebuilt entrance to the Kingsway Subway under Sir Giles Gilbert Scott's planned Waterloo Bridge. Red warning flags protect the roadworks, as a London Transport official stands, with arms apart, in an attempt to control the motor traffic in the main carriageway. A tram on route 72 waits, ready to take passengers right across South London to Beresford Square, Woolwich. C.Klapper/ Omnibus Society

When winter arrived with an icy blast, then the tramlines had to be kept clear by snowploughs such as car 024, depicted here on Victoria Embankment. Lack of evidence of other road vehicles is probably due to the fact that this was a wartime scene – private motoring had virtually ceased due to petrol rationing, and no bus routes ran in this location. One hopes that somewhere inside 024 is a flask full of hot tea for the two brave souls trying to dig a path through the blizzard!

Public transport provision for Wednesday, 12th May 1937, Coronation Day, was displayed on this map issued by London Transport. Tram routes are listed in blue and bus routes appear in red. The busmen, however, were on strike at the time, putting even more pressure on the trams.

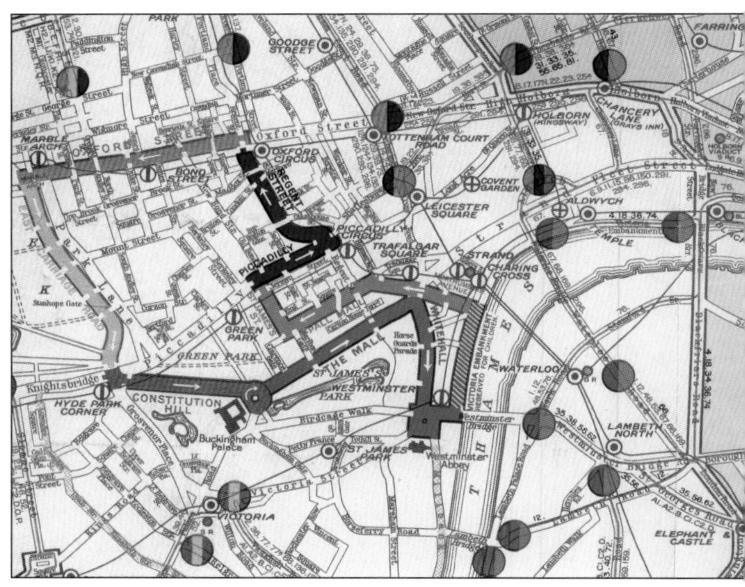

from 27th September to 5th October 1919, brought unheard of crowds on to the Embankment. By this time the LCC were experimenting with unpowered trailer cars attached to some regular service trams, and these coupled sets certainly helped shift the masses who were temporarily barred from using Charing Cross Station.

Trams were missing from the Embankment during the General Strike of May 1926, but otherwise they continued to work hard – unhindered, except by the actions of the elements. On 6th January 1928, the combination of a wind, rain and high tide caused widespread disruption. Floodwater cascaded across the Embankment forcing several motormen to bring their charges to a halt. Stranded vehicles were later hitched to lorries and were unceremoniously towed away back to the depot. At one stage, according to a contemporary newspaper report there were 'miniature waterfalls at Cleopatra's Needle and the RAF Memorial, and the training ship *President* floated at street level'.

The next event to affect services was a major reconstruction project centred on the rebuilding of the Kingsway Subway. This closed to single deck cars on 2nd February 1930, and was reopened for double deck vehicles on 14th January 1931. The opportunity was also taken to refurbish the two intermediate tram stations at Holborn and Aldwych. It was now possible for passengers waiting on the Embankment to catch a tram to places north of the river such as Highgate, Manor House, Hackney and Leyton. The new services were particularly popular with MPs after late night sittings in the House of Commons.

These same Members of Parliament formed part of the loyal assembly of citizens at the coronation of King George VI and Queen Elizabeth. Prior to the actual event preparations had been going ahead to decorate the procession route with flags and bunting. The Victoria Embankment was reserved for schoolchildren, who arrived in their thousands on Wednesday, 12th May 1937. Trams bringing this youthful cargo were stationed in lines north of Hungerford Bridge. Service cars on routes 4, 18, 36 and 74 were cut short to terminate opposite Somerset House and Temple Underground Station. Kingsway Subway trams did not emerge on to the Embankment, but ran as far as Aldwych Station. According to reports the whole occasion went off as planned, the only fly in the ointment was the complete absence of bus services – all the crews had withdrawn their labour!

Although the LCC trams seemed a permanent feature in the London landscape, the writing was already on the wall for this form of transport. At the beginning of the 1930s and throughout that decade efforts were made to replace the railbound vehicles by a more modern and 'attractive' alternative. The favourite in this respect was the trolleybus, which could utilise the tramway electrical infrastructure, but dispensed with the need for a costly permanent way laid in the street. With all this in mind, the planners at 55 Broadway, headquarters of the London Passenger Transport Board, drew up a scheme to abandon all of

Coronation Day, 12th May 1937, saw the arrival of tramloads of schoolchildren intent on securing their allotted place on the procession route. A double line of trams is positioned just in front of Cleopatra's Needle. A group of schoolgirls remains aloof on the left of the picture, while the boys are all marched off in classic crocodile formation. This segregation mirrored LCC instructions. Administrators were also at pains not to place pupils from Roman Catholic schools next to Protestant children from C of E establishments! LCC

London's tramways including the stretches along the Embankment and through the Kingsway Subway.

Predictably, a 'charm offensive' to convince the elected members of the cities of London and Westminster of the merits of the trolleybus was a miserable failure. The prospect of poles and overhead wires obscuring the vista along the Embankment and over Westminster Bridge brought a storm of protest. Then the quibbling began. The big guns were rolled out for both sides. An article in TRANSPORT WORLD for 20th March 1937 took stock of the situation. It quoted the arguments put forward to a Select Committee of the House of Commons:

Westminster City Council objected to trolley vehicles being run along the Victoria Embankment. If the Council succeeded in that opposition, a large part of the trolleybus conversion

These potential victims of London Transport's Trolleybus conversion scheme were to receive an unexpected stay of execution due to the outbreak of World War II. In the foreground a tram on route 35 to Highgate will shortly depart in the direction of the Kingsway Subway, while a stream of sister vehicles wait to gather up and transport the rush hour crowds homewards. LT Museum

scheme would be ruled out because the Embankment was an integral part of many routes south of the river . . .

Mr Frank Pick (vice chairman of the Board) gave evidence in support of the Bill. He said the present proposal covered 132 miles of tramways. About 70 or 80 miles of those routes depended on trolleybuses using the Embankment . . .

It would be essential to have turning points on the Embankment. To run every vehicle the whole length of the Embankment would be wasteful.

Mr F. G. Rye (chairman of the Law and Parliamentary Committee of the Westminster City Council) said the Council opposed because amenities would be interfered with by the overhead equipment (This statement by the learned chairman is remarkably disingenuous bearing in mind the street lights along the Embankment were suspended above the road by means of overhead wires – author) *and because there would be traffic difficulties.*

Mr J. Rawlinson (city engineer, Westminster City Council) said that a census taken on 4th March showed that 1,391 tramcars went on to the Embankment between 8am and 8pm. If they gave way to trolleybuses it would mean an addition of 17 per cent to the general stream of traffic on the Embankment. The turning of trolley vehicles as a matter of daily routine would cause serious interference with traffic.

After recalling Frank Pick to give supplementary evidence, the Select Committee decided very reluctantly to support the introduction of trolleybuses along the Embankment. However, turning circles enabling vehicles to cross the carriageway were taboo at this time. It is interesting to note that two years later the Board did manage to convince the powers that be of the necessity of a least two loops, one by Temple Station and the other opposite Northumberland Avenue. As it was, all these best laid plans came to nought, when the outbreak of the Second World War brought a halt to the south London trolleybus conversion programme.

The Blitz and the sustained bombing of 1940/41 caused many disruptions across a wide area of the metropolis. Things were no different along the Embankment, where a number of incidents were recorded. On Monday 9th September 1940, enemy raiders struck at the St Thomas's Hospital/Westminster Bridge junction causing suspension of tram services. The next day, several high explosive bombs fell on the Embankment severing tram tracks and damaging Charing Cross Station. By 18th September engineers had managed to construct temporary tram bridges to span the bomb craters.

It was the Kingsway Subway's turn on 20th November, when extensive damage was caused to the area round the southern portal. Water and gas mains were also destroyed in the attack, and normal service through the subway could only resume on 18th December. Worse was to follow at the end of the year, when on 30th December concerted incendiary bomb attacks on the centre of London closed Blackfriars Bridge and the Victoria Embankment as far down as Somerset House. Fire brigade hoses taking water from the Thames straddled the highway, thus halting all traffic. A solitary tram, burnt out by an incendiary, was noted at the Westminster Bridge end of the Embankment.

The new year of 1941 brought more death and destruction. On Tuesday, 14th January, Blackfriars Bridge was closed for 24 hours while bomb damage was being repaired. A respite of sorts intervened until the spring, when on 17th April an explosion damaged Hungerford Bridge and was also the cause of a large hole in the Embankment. Tram services were diverted to terminate either side of Somerset House, and this situation lasted a week until new track spanned the bomb crater.

One final attempt by the Luftwaffe to cripple London took place over the weekend of 10th/11th May. Incendiaries and high explosive bombs caused havoc and resulted in the Embankment being deprived of trams for many hours. Tracks in all the

THE SCARS THAT DISFIGURE THE PEDESTAL
OF THE OBELISK, THE BASES OF THE SPHINXES
AND THE RIGHT HAND SPHINX WERE CAUSED
BY FRAGMENTS OF A BOMB DROPPED IN THE
ROADWAY CLOSE TO THIS SPOT, IN THE FIRST
RAID ON LONDON BY GERMAN AEROPLANES A
FEW MINUTES BEFORE MIDNIGHT ON TUESDAY
4TH SEPTEMBER 1917

The Victoria Embankment was hit by bombing in both World War I and World War II. The First World War bomb was dropped in the first ever air raid on London and is commemorated on a plaque fixed to the base of one of the Sphinxes. James Whiting

The tramway era is drawing to a close, as we witness trams 1862 and 175 passing outside Westminster passenger shelter. A replacement bus from one of the earlier conversion stages is glimpsed in the distance. The shelter was later torn down, when the junction with Bridge Street was remodelled and the carriageway expanded to cater for the increased traffic.
D.A.Thompson/LCCTT

Repairs are taking place to the front of Unilever House, as tram 1812 waits by the shelter at Blackfriars. In the dappled shade of the plane trees, this is a classic postwar shot, before the upheavals of the 1960s and 1970s, when town planners and highway engineers conspired to 'modernise' this previously untroubled location with the construction of a traffic underpass.

approach streets in South London were blocked by debris or by fire crews endeavouring to stem the tide of destruction. To add to the mayhem, there was also a direct hit on the southern portal of the Kingsway Subway. Trams working from north London could not enter the subway and were forced to turn short at Holborn Hall.

Those hardy souls who did attempt to get to work on Monday 12th May found Westminster Bridge Road impassable. Passengers arriving by tram either had to make a detour via Vauxhall and the Albert Embankment, or they were obliged to take a chance on the northern route via Blackfriars Bridge. Long delays to Embankment bound services were experienced in the Elephant and Castle area as rescue services toiled to clear unsafe buildings and to put out the remaining fires.

Although Londoners were unaware of it at the time, the full force of Nazi aggression had now passed, and in spite of further raids throughout the rest of the war, the situation was never quite as bad as it had been on that weekend in May.

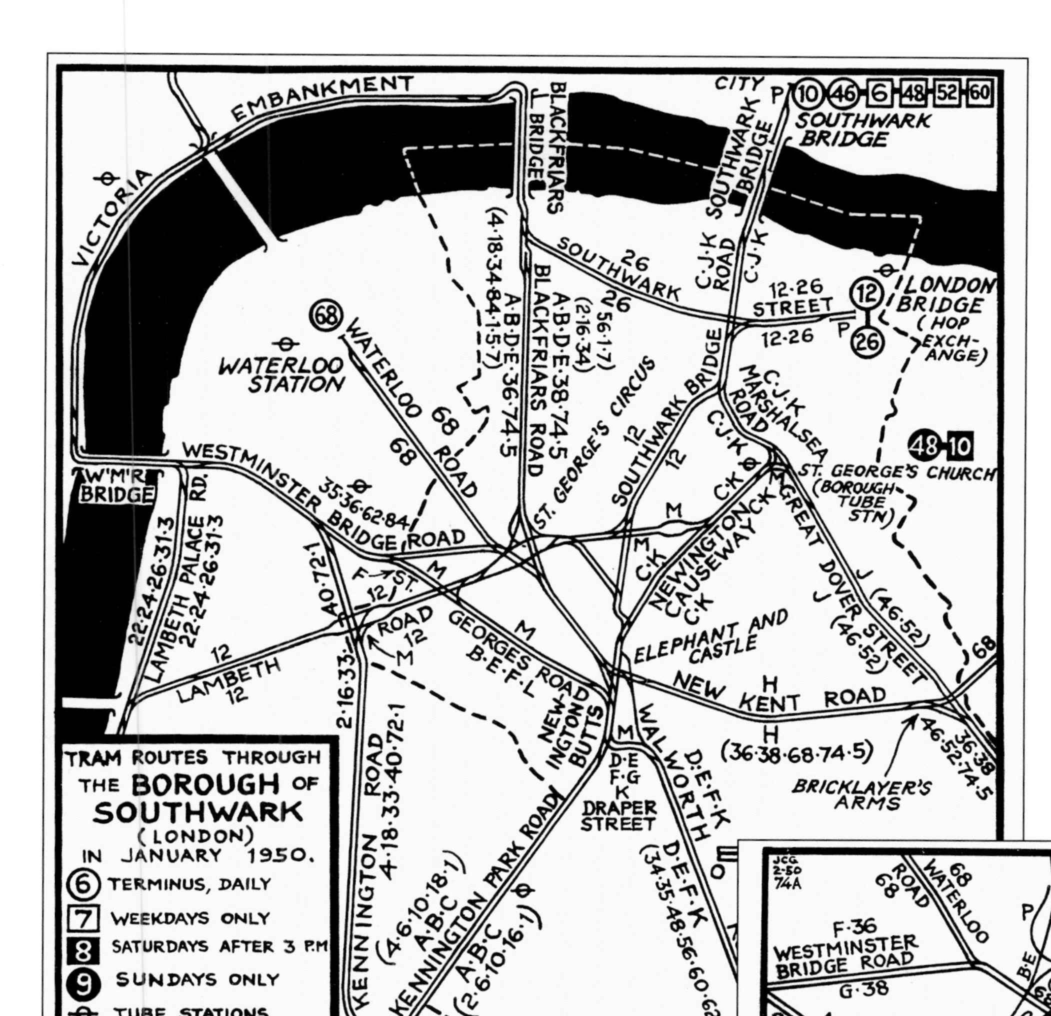

The tramway network leading to the bridges and Victoria Embankment is clearly illustrated in this February 1950 track map. The complexity of the inner south London trackwork contrasts with the simplicity of the Embankment loop and the connection to the Kingsway Subway. John Gillham, who checked every yard of track on the London system, painstakingly collected all the information in this map. Transport historians owe much to John and his meticulous research. J.C.Gillham

Peacetime brought austerity and a slow recovery from the deprivations of the recent conflict. A decision was reached regarding what was left of the London tram system – it would be abandoned in favour of diesel buses. Implementation of the late 1930s trolleybus plans for the Westminster Bridge and Blackfriars areas would not now take place. The two local authorities – Westminster and the City of London – were going to be spared the 'awful prospect' of trolleybus wires lowering the amenity value of the district.

The postwar policy of austerity meant that the carriageway along the Embankment remained a patchwork of varying road surfaces laid to cover the bomb craters. At the side of the main highway, on what was virtually a private right of way, maintenance on the tram tracks was kept to a minimum level; it was only in 1948/49 that extensive relaying work could be undertaken. Repairs were still needed because, on the section between County Hall, Westminster Bridge and the Kingsway Subway entrance under Waterloo Bridge, there was an intensive service of 226 trams per hour. On the stretch from Savoy Street to Blackfriars the somewhat lower figure of 86 cars an hour still represented an impressive total. This flow of vehicles was interrupted for three days from Friday, 14th July 1950, when the Embankment was temporarily closed at Charing Cross to allow the finishing touches to be applied to the Bailey bridge across the river to the Festival of Britain site on the South Bank. Trams were curtailed at a crossover by New Scotland Yard and at Savoy Street. Kingsway Subway routes 31, 33 and 35, that would normally use Westminster Bridge were obliged to reverse

Trams reversing on the Embankment were an everyday occurrence. Sometimes, vehicles like Feltham car 2098 were turned short on the instructions of an inspector. This practice was meant to regulate the number of trams in order to ensure an efficient service for the travelling public. We are in City of London territory, at the facing crossover by Temple Avenue. A.D.Packer

outside the entrance in order to continue their journeys via Blackfriars Bridge.

However permanent this thriving tramway scene may have appeared to a casual observer, there were changes in the air which would eventually result in the complete eradication of this form of transport. The first blow fell at the end of September 1950, when tram routes in southwest London were axed. Diesel buses then appeared in numbers for the first time on the Embankment. The planners at London Transport did a less than perfect job when they allowed these replacement vehicles to run along part of the tramway. Great care and attention were necessary as bus drivers piloted their charges along the inner tram track nearest to the river. There was precious little room to spare between the new buses and the old trams. Sceptics rightly pointed out that this arrangement constituted 'an accident about to happen' and in this they were to be proved correct. After several comparatively minor scrapes,

On 3rd November 1950, tram 192 derailed just opposite Big Ben. Luckily, the tram stayed upright and there were no serious casualties among the passengers and crew. Representatives of the rescue services attending the incident include an LCC Daimler ambulance and London Transport breakdown tender 177K. The latter will probably have to effect the removal of the stricken tramcar. Single line working was in force for trams entering and leaving the Embankment, until the debris could be cleared and the rails in the foreground checked by the permanent way department.

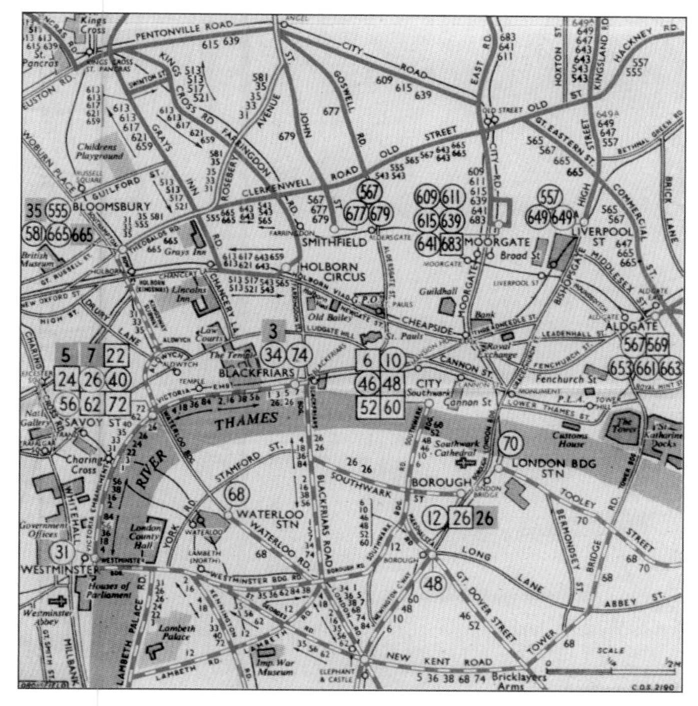

This central London extract from the January 1950 Tram & Trolleybus Map shows the important position of the Victoria Embankment in the network.

a serious collision occurred on 11th September 1951, when an eastbound tram on route 56 hit a bus on route 170.

The tram replacement programme continued unabated until the final day – Saturday 5th July 1952. The obsequies had actually started earlier in the week, as visitors to the capital and those curious to witness the end of an era swelled the numbers of people on the Embankment. On the final evening of tramway operation most vehicles were packed to the gunwales as they passed along the tracks for the last time. A favourite way of saying *adieu* was to place pennies on the rails so that the tram wheels could flatten them.

It is recorded that Car 309 left the Victoria Embankment at 11.40pm for the final run to Abbey Wood, thus bringing down the curtain on almost five decades of tramway operation in this part of London.

Tram 116 is depicted here at Westminster, directly opposite the stairs leading to the Underground station. Route 84 had to traverse the steep Dog Kennel Hill in south London to reach the terminus in suburban Peckham Rye. Even though the trams were officially on their way out, this vehicle still looks capable of many more years of faithful service. F.W. Ivey

Chapter 6 Road Traffic

One of the main functions of the Victoria Embankment is to act as a bypass for traffic wishing to avoid the congested centre of town. Surveys conducted in Victorian times revealed an alarming state of affairs. Already, by 1855, a staggering 200,000 people a day were recorded as having passed along the roads between Charing Cross and the City.

Unfortunately, there hasn't been much improvement in the intervening century and a half. Ask any modern day London cabbie the quickest way from the Houses of Parliament to the City of London and the reply will refer to the subject of this book. In a taxi it is a straightforward journey along the A3211 Victoria Embankment to Blackfriars, and then via Upper Thames Street into the heart of the Square Mile. This avoids all the congestion associated with the historic 'direct route' which traverses Whitehall, the Strand, Fleet Street and Ludgate Hill.

Motorists nowadays are not likely to be at all interested in

We go back to a time when pedestrians could amble gently across Victoria Embankment secure in the knowledge that they would be very unlikely to come to grief. A line of cabs waits to the left of the picture, while a single horse van heads a procession of other slow moving vehicles. There hardly seems to be a need for the island refuge equipped with a solitary gas lamp.

what lies beneath their vehicles. Only when cones and temporary traffic lights appear on the scene to cordon off 'yet another lot of roadworks', will the essential maintenance of the highway come to mind – and then not in a very complimentary light. Yet, it is worth recounting some facts concerning the basics of the Victoria Embankment.

When the thoroughfare opened in 1870, the road surface owed much to the pioneering work of J. L. MacAdam (1756–1836). His contribution to the science of highway engineering would earn him the gratitude of generations of road users and town planners. He took coal tar – a byproduct of the town gas industry – and combined it with graded stones. This hot mixture was subsequently applied onto the stone foundation of the Embankment. The surface was then rolled flat and finished with a fine layer of sand. In this state, the recently laid waterbound macadam roadway was fit to receive the attentions of the horse drawn traffic of the day.

As with all new technologies, the macadam method was not without its critics. They took exception to the fact that the road was liable to become muddy in winter and dusty in summer. Granite setts and wood block paving gave a hardwearing surface and were extensively used throughout the capital. When it was suggested that the Embankment be treated in the same way, local politicians blanched at the cost of the project.

In the first decade of the twentieth century it became increasingly apparent that the internal combustion engine was here to stay. Motorised vehicles were appearing in growing numbers and the effect of their wheels on the waterbound macadam was very damaging. Clearly, a solution had to be found, and pressure on the members of the LCC Highways Committee resulted in trials being conducted. During 1906/7, sections of the Embankment were either treated with compounds of tar macadam or were surfaced with bitumen based asphalt macadam. Different companies were allotted separate stretches of the road, so that quality control tests could be carried out. With the speed, volume and weight of traffic increasing annually, it did not take long to determine that asphalt was the clear winner, and in 1909 the whole contract was awarded to the Trinidad Lake Asphalt Company. Both the wearing surface and the base course of the carriageway were constructed using a mixture of Fluxed Trinidad Lake Asphalt, Portland Cement, sand and crushed Guernsey granite. This process was applied to the whole width of the carriageway, with the exception of the tram tracks, which were paved with Aberdeen granite setts.

The Trinidad Company was so pleased with the results that it later publicised the fact that no major resurfacing work had been necessary for well over forty years after the initial contract was completed. There must have been some truth in these

Even after the trams arrived in 1906, the horse still reigned supreme. We can observe the horse drawn dray with the driver, his whip at his side. The two motor cars, heading for Blackfriars, still seem out of place. Note the poor road surface nearest the landward kerb, and the granite setts adjacent to the tramway.

Around 1913, when this view was taken, the internal combustion engine began to make its presence felt on the streets of London. Away from the Embankment, petrol driven motor buses already dominated the scene. They shared road space with a variety of taxicabs, delivery vans and steam lorries. The ability of a pedestrian to stroll nonchalantly across the road now looks in doubt.
J.B.Gent Collection

claims, because Westminster City Council and the City of London Corporation came knocking on the same company's door in 1952, after the London trams had breathed their last. A scheme was worked out for the complete reconstruction of the Embankment into a dual carriageway with two 28 feet (8.5 metres) wide roadways separated by a 6 feet (1.8 metres) wide central reservation. Sensibly, in view of the disruption likely to be caused by the forthcoming Coronation procession route, the start date was fixed at September 1953 – a good thirteen months after the last tram and two months after the Coronation. As a temporary expedient the tram rails and the conduit slots had been covered with strips of asphalt.

In many parts of London, tramlines left redundant by the prewar trolleybus conversion programme remained concealed under a new road surface. However tracks abandoned throughout south London in the early 1950s were lifted so that the scrap value could be realised on the rails, points and crossings. This approach was adopted along the Embankment, where the site of the old tramway was filled with hardcore and concrete. The opportunity was also taken to install new gullies, drain connections and electric cable ducts. Differences in carriageway and footpath levels had to be tackled, and the problem was partly solved by constructing a raft of concrete, six inches (152mm) thick, along the complete length of the old tram tracks. The final asphalt surface was laid mechanically by several Barber-Greene finishers. The Embankment was one of the first major roads in the centre of London to incorporate a continuous non-skid surface. The whole project was completed by May 1954.

Having a splendidly paved avenue in the centre of London was of little value at night if road users couldn't see where they were going! The provision of street lighting had concerned Sir Joseph Bazalgette since the opening of the Embankment.

Members of the Metropolitan Board of Works, who had travelled to the Paris Exhibition of 1878, came back impressed with the use of electric lighting along the Avenue de l'Opéra. The installation was the work of a Russian engineer, Paul Jablochkoff (1847–1894). He had invented an arc lamp known as the Jablochkoff Candle, which produced a much brighter light than contemporary gas lamps. A small generating station was installed on the Embankment to power twenty of the Jablochkoff lights, and the installation was switched on in December 1878. Such was the immediate success with the general public that the whole thoroughfare from Westminster to Blackfriars was soon basking in artificial illumination. It was claimed that the Victoria Embankment was the first street in Great Britain to be lit by electricity. The whole spectacle was the wonder of the age, and the very favourable public response prompted the City of London to copy the MBW's initiative by using the new technology at the Mansion House, Billingsgate Fish Market and along the Holborn Viaduct. Unfortunately, the novelty of the experiment was tarnished somewhat when the bills started to roll in! Doubts were also expressed concerning the reliability and durability of the equipment. In the event, the Jablochkoff Company later went bankrupt and gas lighting was reinstated from June 1884.

Such was the disappointing outcome to Sir Joseph's visionary innovation. Jablochkoff paid the price of a pioneer. After the great switch off, the Embankment reverted to nighttime gloom, with only gas lamps to penetrate the swirling London fogs. Carters and cab drivers were not slow in expressing a preference for using the alternative route via the Strand. They felt safer mingling with the rest of humanity. When dusk fell, a trip along the Embankment in the last decade of the nineteenth century could be a faintly unearthly experience, punctuated by the appearance of ghostly figures darting across the road or by lights from the odd passing river vessel. This romantic ambiance may have been fine for artists, poets, courting couples and people of the night who didn't wish to be disturbed, but the newspapers and the Metropolitan Police were not happy. The latter had adopted a 'get tough policy' on down-and-outs, who congregated around Charing Cross and Hungerford Bridge, and constables regularly complained that 'not being able to see where they were going' hampered them in their duties

The whole matter of street lighting finally surfaced again at a meeting of the LCC Highways Committee in July 1895. A sum of £16,590 was proposed to restore the road to its pre-1884 brilliance, and, from then until the blackout of the Second World War, complaints about the gloom subsided. As an aside to all this – when the lights did go up again, the tramps simply thumbed their noses at the Metropolitan Police and adopted a diversionary tactic by crossing the boundary at the Temple, where the City of London Police adopted a more liberal approach to their activities!

Of course, the Metropolitan Police Commissioner had more weighty affairs on his mind than chasing vagrants about. He was in charge of an organisation responsible for the smooth running of London's traffic, and as such, the replacement of the horse by the internal combustion engine simply added to his troubles. He was not short of advice from various pressure groups. A typical example is quoted in the THIRD ANNUAL REPORT OF THE LONDON AND HOME COUNTIES TRAFFIC ADVISORY COMMITTEE FOR 1927–28:

We are invited by the London County Council to state our views on a proposal made by the Automobile Association for the adoption on the Victoria Embankment of the principle that traffic should be kept to the right of red reflex discs, and to the left of white reflex discs, to be erected for this purpose, and the Association offered to provide the necessary discs for fixing on the guard posts of the refuges. After consideration of the legal and traffic aspects of the question, we considered that the proposal would be likely to lead to difficulties in application especially on a thoroughfare so heavily trafficked as the Embankment where the conditions are somewhat abnormal by reason of the position of the tramway track, and therefore recommend that the proposal should not be accepted.

The 'heavily trafficked' aspect of the Embankment was not helped by the appearance of the odd speedster, confident in the belief that practice made perfect before applying to compete in the British Grand Prix. In 1938, national sporting hero, Captain George Eyston, made headlines by being stopped for driving in excess of the 30mph limit. Whether the speed ace, more often associated with the Brooklands Race Track, momentarily confused the Embankment with the Bonneville Salt Flats, we shall never know. Perhaps the euphoria of shooting across Utah and creating a new world land speed record of 357mph had gone to his head. Luckily, no pedestrians trying to cross from Northumberland Avenue to the bank of the Thames were mowed down in the attempt.

One of the police's other concerns was the licensing of public service vehicles – omnibuses, cabs and tramcars. However, whenever a guardian of the public peace looked out from his office in New Scotland Yard, there would have been scant evidence of omnibuses, horse drawn or otherwise, using the Victoria Embankment on a regular basis. This was the situation for many decades. A list of London horse bus services for 1895 implies that all vehicles navigated their way via the Strand and Whitehall. When all is said and done, the paying customers wanted to be dropped off by 'the shops and the bright lights', all of which were very much absent along the Embankment.

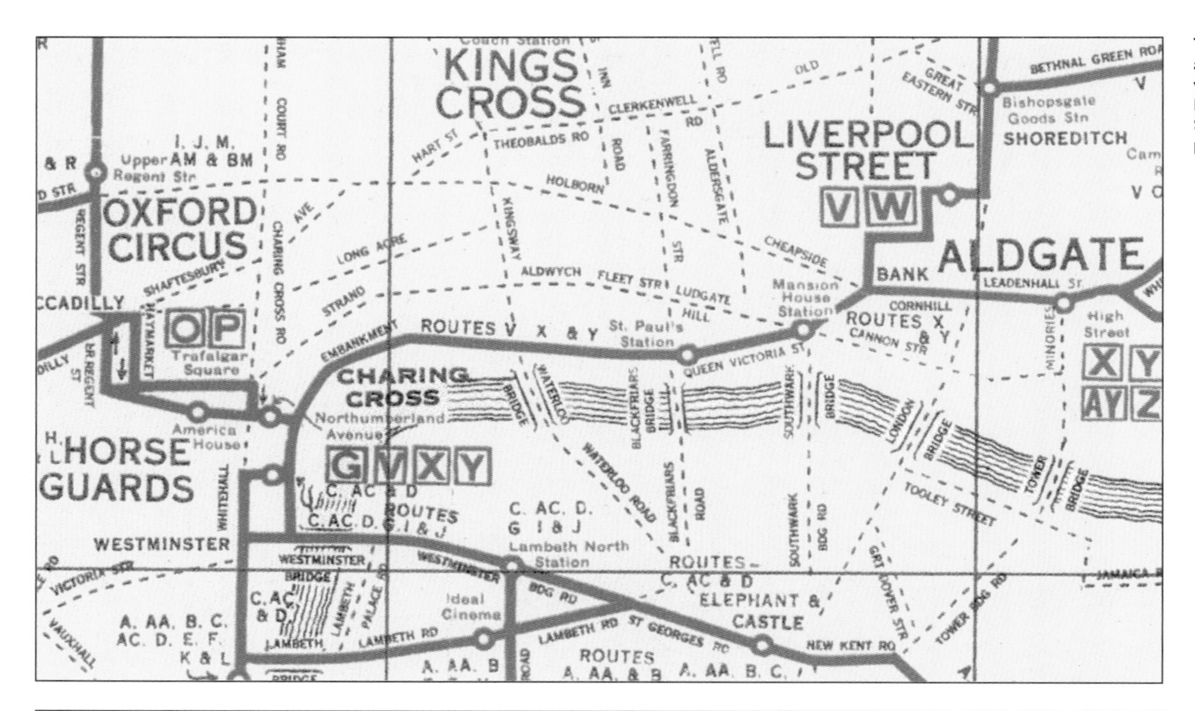

This Green Line map is an extract from a larger version contained in the London Transport Second Annual Report published in 1935.

In the early 1930s, Green Line coaches were frequent visitors to the Embankment – by October 1932, no fewer than five routes terminated at Charing Cross. AEC Green Line coach T186 heads a queue of vehicles waiting to depart to their respective outer suburban termini.
Omnibus Society

Subsequent bus timetables, issued during the motorised era, reinforce the belief that the London General Omnibus Company, its competitors and its successors regarded the road from Westminster to Blackfriars as pure tram territory. The 1924 General Bus Map records six routes using Westminster Bridge, with the same number traversing Waterloo Bridge, and five routes crossing into the City by means of Blackfriars Bridge. On one of the first London Transport maps of 1934, the total number of routes passing over Westminster and Waterloo bridges had risen to eleven for each. It goes without saying that along Whitehall, through Trafalgar Square, past the front of Charing Cross Station and down the Strand there were buses galore.

The message was clear – if you wanted to hop on a bus anywhere on the Embankment, you might have a very long wait. However, this wasn't always the case and it sometimes happened that, in the case of accidents, state processions, bomb alerts or monster political marches, bus services were temporarily diverted by way of Horse Guards Avenue or Northumberland Avenue. This operational necessity continues to the present day, and buses unable to enter Parliament Square or parts of Whitehall may find themselves directed to emergency stops on the Victoria Embankment. In fact, for many years, a very discreet motor bus presence was maintained in the area by the operation of several Green Line coach services. The 1938 GREEN LINE COACH GUIDE, published by London Transport, lists two stops in Northumberland Avenue and two in Horse Guards Avenue. From the latter, travellers could reach a range of destinations including Tunbridge Wells, Westerham, Windsor, Farnham Common and Burnham Beeches.

Green Line routes V, X and Y, serving the outer termini of Bishops Stortford, Brentwood and Gidea Park respectively, traversed most of the length of the Embankment in order to finish their journeys at Northumberland Avenue. The introduction of the winter timetable, on 6th October 1937, saw their withdrawal from Victoria Embankment.

Accidents will happen! The EVENING NEWS for 11th September 1951 carried this picture of an unfortunate contretemps between an RTL bus and a tramcar. Mixed operation of trams and buses along the Embankment brought many headaches for London Transport officials. Recently trained bus drivers had to be adept at steering and tramway motormen had to have quick reactions in using the magnetic brakes.

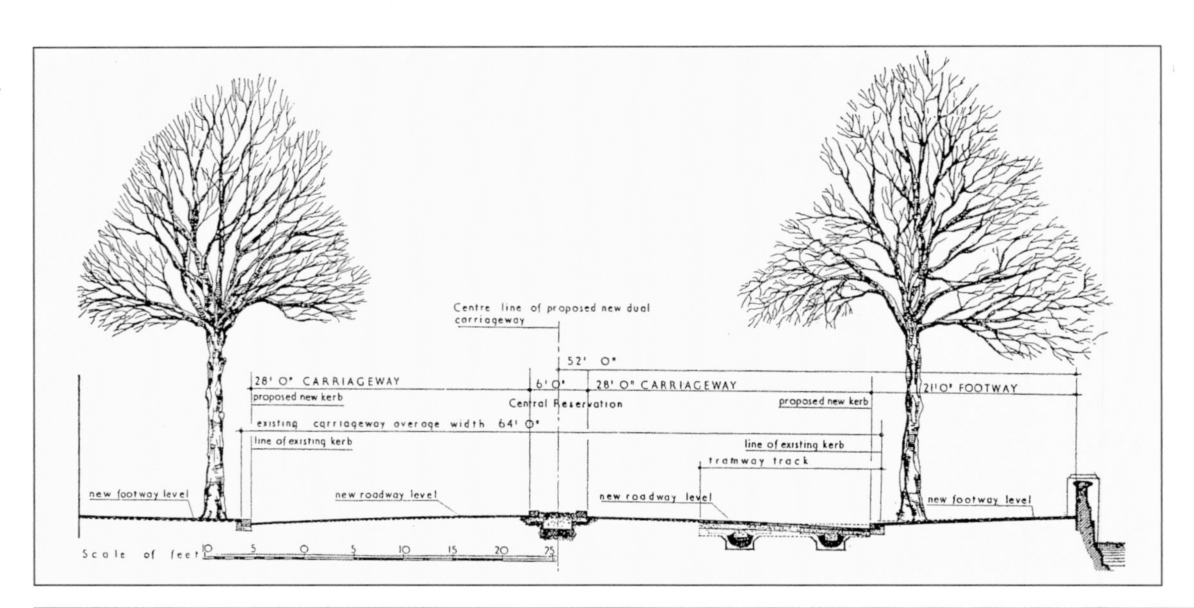

This cross section diagram was prepared for the reconstruction of the carriageway after the trams were abandoned.

After the festivities connected with the Coronation of Queen Elizabeth II were concluded, contractors descended on the Embankment to remove the tram tracks and reinstate the roadway. This view was taken on 13th September 1953. It presents a sad sight to any tramway enthusiast, as a mechanical claw tears through the infrastructure, so carefully designed by a past generation of LCC engineers. Metal poles and iron stakes driven into the road surface do the job that would be filled nowadays by plastic traffic cones. J.C.Gillham

A time span lasting three decades accounted for the arrival of the traditional London red bus along the Embankment and its demise. Route 168 dated from 1st October 1950 – the day it replaced tram service 26. The driver of RTL 1135 finds himself in a tight situation as he endeavours to manoeuvre his vehicle into the space left between tram 1890 and the kerb. This route used a new bus terminal stand in Horse Guards Avenue, but the arrangement was never a convenient one. Other potential termini for buses replacing trams, such as Temple Place, failed to gain approval from the local authority. C.Carter

As has already been noted in the tramway chapter, construction of the new Waterloo Bridge resulted in the rebuilding of the southern portal to the Kingsway Tram Subway. This was regarded by officials at London Transport as a temporary state of affairs, until all tram routes running along the Embankment could be ousted. The urgent matter of the conversion of the subway to trolleybus or bus operation resurfaced after the war. In a series of letters emanating from the office of P. Croom-Johnson, Chief Engineer to London Transport, various options were discussed.

It is clear from the outset that, by 1945, buses were preferred to trolleybuses; therefore, attention had to be paid to ventilating the subway in order to remove exhaust gases. Because the height of vehicles ruled out overhead ducting, fumes would have to be expelled via a system of masonry ducts. These would take the place of the tramway conduits beneath each 'bus track'. Forced ventilation would be effected by means of fan equipped shafts leading to the surface. The proposed positioning of these vents was discussed with representatives from the London County Council. They seem to have been lukewarm as to the project, and it was generally agreed that permission for a large fan chamber and associated ducting outside the Embankment portal would not be granted.

Two estimates were prepared: Scheme 2, which was for a tunnel to serve bus traffic in both directions, was costed at £579,500. Scheme 3, for the tunnel to accommodate southbound traffic only, came out at around £140,000. Following this set of costings, the subject of running buses through the Kingsway Subway quietly died a death. A brief flurry of activity occurred at the end of 1954, when J.Boyd-Carpenter, the Minister of Transport, announced that it would cost £175,000 to convert the subway into a car park. This proposal was deemed too expensive.

When the project to convert the subway for road traffic was resurrected in the 1960s, a shorter, one way underpass was incorporated into part of the original tram tunnel. However, the entrance for road traffic was not situated on the Embankment, but was constructed in Lancaster Place; the exit was on the site of the former Aldwych Tram Station, at the southern end of Kingsway.

When diesel buses finally did appear in numbers on Victoria Embankment, this was as a direct result of the 1950–52 tramway conversion programme. Ironically, although the big wigs at 55 Broadway were keen to rid themselves of their railbound embarrassments, they still thought in tramlines! Instead of being integrated into the existing network, most of the replacing buses stuck rigidly to the Embankment loop principle, so beloved of the LCC Tramways. The 1953 bus map lists no fewer than thirteen services; these also included the three routes which were substituted for the Kingsway Subway trams. Instead of running through the subway, routes 170, 171 and 172 were diverted to serve Temple Place, Arundel Street and Norfolk Street. In addition there were four night bus routes. In two short years, the Embankment had gone from being an omnibus desert to a veritable cornucopia of diesels, predominantly of the RT and RTL types.

Car parking outside the Embankment Gardens wasn't a problem in the early 1960s. Shell Mex House and the Savoy form the backdrop to this view, taken in an era when private motoring was beginning to make serious inroads into public transport passenger levels. R.J. Harley

However, this state of plenty didn't last long. Like victims in some bizarre London Transport murder mystery, these newly introduced bus routes were gradually bumped off one by one. Official reasons for the 'Great Embankment Bus Massacre' centred on changing travel patterns and the need for efficiency. It was already apparent during tram days that, outside peak hours, the number of passengers being carried along the Embankment was very low. The introduction of the five day office working week had also made inroads into passenger loadings for Saturday mornings and lunchtimes. Extra services were now unnecessary. The practice of parking buses on the landward side of the Embankment also ceased. This had probably been a fuel economy measure to save vehicles, used in the morning and evening peaks, from making empty return journeys back to the bus garage.

In the fifties and sixties the lure of the private motor car had become irresistible for thousands of former bus passengers. London Transport had to respond to a situation that was made worse by a crippling bus strike in 1958.

From the late 1950s onwards traffic congestion began to disrupt timetables. Whereas trams had had the Embankment to themselves, buses had to compete for road space with every other motorised Tom, Dick and Harry. Peak hour tailbacks grew at every junction and at every set of traffic lights. Sometimes it was quicker to walk than to remain sitting in a bus stuck in a jam. The net result of all this was a situation with which we are familiar today.

The loss of bus route 104 – Tooting to Victoria Embankment (Horse Guards Avenue) – on 30th April 1958, marked the start of a planned route withdrawal process. Throughout the sixties and seventies the casualty list lengthened, as buses were either withdrawn north of the Elephant and Castle or were diverted to run via Whitehall and the Strand. Certain peak hour journeys of route 184 soldiered on until 11th July 1992, when the Central Bus era effectively ended along the Victoria Embankment. Henceforth, the familiar London double decker bus, aside from the occasional tourist vehicle, would become somewhat of a *rara avis* at this location. At the time of writing, only the night bus service N50 uses the road on its journey from Trafalgar Square to East Beckton.

The area is now well within the Congestion Charge Zone of central London, and thus any private motorist must now pay extra on a weekday for the privilege of driving along the Embankment. Metered parking spaces are provided, but on Mondays to Fridays can be used after 10am only. To draw motorists' attention to this, the meters are painted white. You can still take a cab, of course.

Since around 1907, motorised taxicabs have been appearing on the streets of London, and their successors still roar past pedestrians with the best of them. Perhaps the fate of Captain George Eyston still stands as a salutary lesson to those who wish to outwit the latest Metropolitan Police road safety speed cameras!

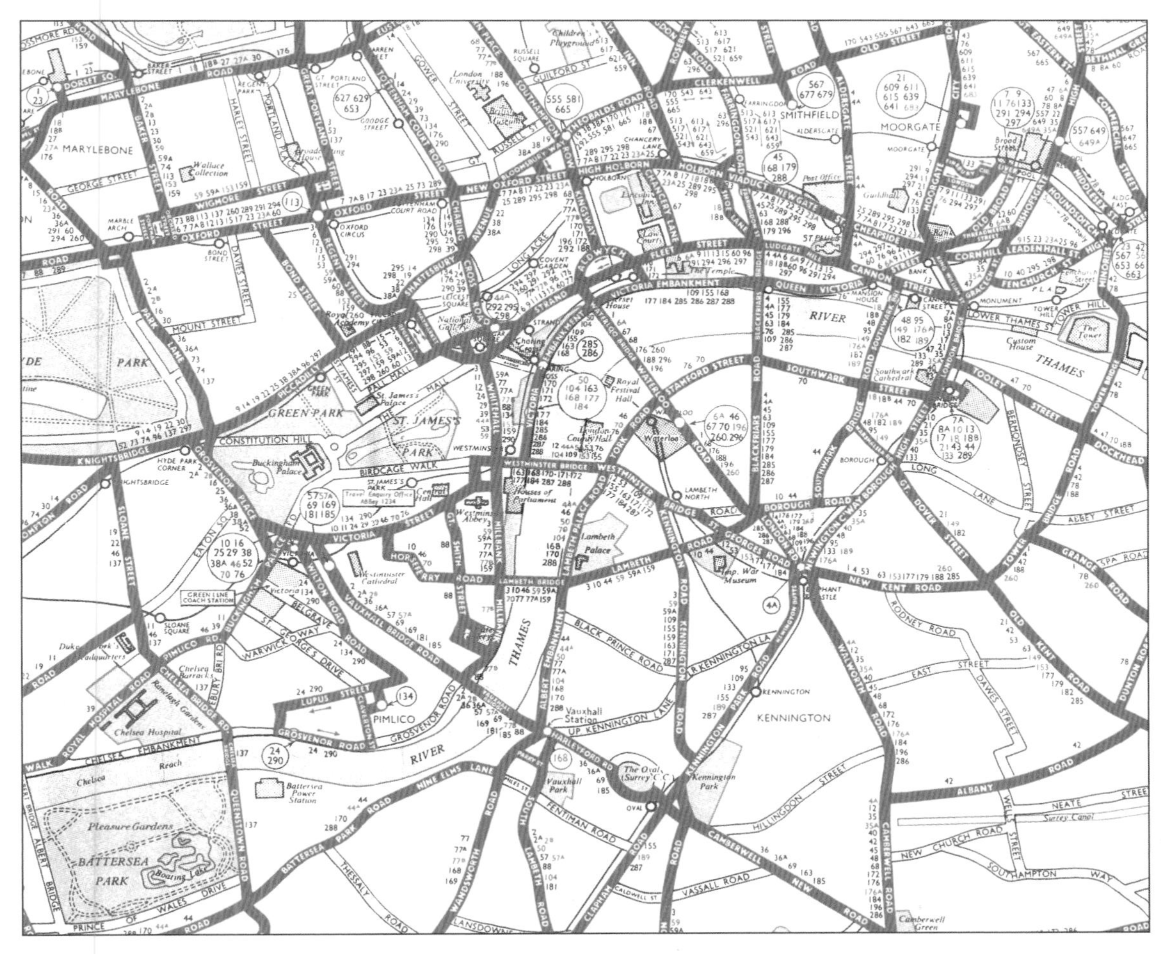

The 1957 Central Bus & Trolleybus Map still includes a full complement of routes serving Victoria Embankment – some of which terminated at Horse Guards Avenue.

Today, no ordinary bus services run along Victoria Embankment. In this view, one of the feared inspectors of the Red Route Patrol emerges from his vehicle, just as a London tourist bus speeds past. Even in winter – this view was taken in February 2004 – some passengers have braved the cold to sit on the (mainly open) top deck of the Big Bus Company's vehicle. Victoria Embankment provides a relatively uncongested run for the bus, due no doubt to the efforts of the Red Route Patrol in deterring errant motorists!
R.J. Harley

Chapter 7 WESTMINSTER BRIDGE

THE OFT quoted line "Earth has not anything to show more fair . . . " has also been mercilessly parodied. No more so than at the time of the great smog of December 1952, when thousands of Londoners were literally choking on atmospheric pollution, which was then doing its level best to stifle the life out of the capital. The lofty sentiments with which the poet, William Wordsworth, greeted the morning of 3rd September 1802 from his vantage point on Westminster Bridge, have secured a place in the canon of Romantic literature. The poem paints a wonderful picture of a city "All bright and glittering in the smokeless air"; the whole work has secured lasting immortality for the particular river crossing that is the subject of this chapter.

Aside from the glories of Wordsworth's masterpiece, one of the major attributes of Westminster Bridge in the artistic and literary world has always been as a lead-in or a foreground feature to a backdrop of architectural splendour. Unfairly, the structure of the bridge itself seems to pale into insignificance when contrasted to the instantly recognisable silhouette of Big Ben and the Houses of Parliament. In short, it has always

This print was produced just after the completion of the 'new' Westminster Bridge. Notwithstanding the state of the murky waters, there seems to be a lively group of vessels plying their trade. In time honoured fashion, the crew of the Thames Barge has lowered the main mast before passing under one of the arches of the new bridge. R.J. Harley Collection

This engraving is dated 11th June 1864 and represents the proposed design of Westminster Pier before the actual Embankment was built. Nevertheless, many of the features shown here survived to be incorporated in the completed Victoria Embankment. The seemingly tranquil scene belied the fact that the river was heavily polluted with effluent. Note that one of the steam boats has lowered its chimney to pass under one of the arches of the new bridge, just as sailing barges would lower their main masts. Guildhall Library

played a supporting role on the tourist circuit and on countless postcard views taken from the South Bank looking towards Westminster.

The history of the bridge begins with public agitation for a new crossing of the Thames that would relieve the congested bottleneck of London Bridge. The £390,000 cost of Westminster Bridge was partly funded from lottery money and partly from the national exchequer. Construction commenced in 1739 and finished in 1747, after which there was a delay of three years because one of the stone piers was found to be unsafe due to subsidence. As it turned out, this was an unfortunate omen for the future. Swiss engineer Charles Labelye designed the first Westminster Bridge, and under his guidance, workmen produced what has been described as 'a handsome edifice' of fifteen stone arches, which supported a roadway 1,160 feet (353.5 metres) long and 43 feet (13.1 metres) wide. For many years the bridge performed its function well. As it was not subject to a toll, it was especially popular with Londoners. In inclement weather travellers could take advantage of regularly placed, domed, octagonal refuges at the bridge piers. These were fairly safe during daylight hours, but gained an unsavoury reputation after dusk, when the eighteenth century equivalent of muggers took up residence. Fortunately the authorities responded by posting twelve night watchmen in an attempt to minimise the risk of innocent pedestrians being beaten up, robbed and then thrown in the Thames!

During the first four decades of the nineteenth century, the state of the bridge deteriorated to such an extent that drastic action had to be taken to lighten the weight of the structure. Redundant stonework was sacrificed in the forlorn hope that

The original lamps on the bridge have now been altered to a more elaborate design, in keeping with prevailing Victorian taste. Traffic is solely equine powered, and it will take the imminent arrival of electric tramways to change the status quo. A solitary horse bus makes its way towards the Houses of Parliament and the West End.

the piers of the bridge would cease their slow, but relentless descent into the river bed. Half the bridge ended up being supported by timber struts and braces, but these temporary measures could not halt the inevitable decision to knock down Labelye's handiwork and replace it with a new river crossing. This course of action to go ahead with the demolition was taken in 1846 and immediately provoked opposition from the heritage lobby and the aesthetes of the day. No doubt, they wanted to preserve Wordsworth's literary stone monument for posterity. More prosaically, none of the critics could suggest a viably sound engineering solution to stop the sinking bridge. Therefore, it was time to wipe the slate clean, and work finally began in 1854 on the construction of the second Westminster Bridge, which we all know today.

The transition period took some time as dismantling of the old and construction of the new proceeded in tandem. Some houses on the Surrey side of the river had to be pulled down because of the need for an improved alignment of wider approach roads. The old bridge finally disappeared in 1861, having eked out its last months as a pedestrian only thoroughfare.

The official opening of the new bridge, constructed to the designs of Thomas Page, occurred on Saturday 24th May 1862. It was the same length as its predecessor, but was built slightly further north. The replacement could now boast a total width of 85 feet (25.9 metres), of which the carriageway, capable of carrying six lanes of traffic, took up 58 feet (17.6 metres) – a more than adequate space to cope with the prevailing stream of mid-Victorian vehicles. The span of the central arch was 120 feet (36.5 metres), with maximum headroom of 19 feet 6 inches (5.9 metres), whilst the other six arches had a span of 114 feet (34.7 metres) each.

Eleven o'clock in the morning; the tower of Big Ben seems to emerge from the top deck of LCC tramcar 851, which has SOMERSET HOUSE on the destination blind. The rest of the traffic, including a couple of taxis, has learnt to take avoiding action and to steer clear of the tram tracks. On the Westminster side of the bridge, a fair queue of vehicles has built up; perhaps the horses are having trouble on the slight gradient leading from Bridge Street. J.B.Gent Collection

Thomas Page wisely consulted with Sir Charles Barry so that the architectural style of the bridge remained in keeping with that of the Houses of Parliament. The final bill came to some quarter of a million pounds, which was rather put into the shade by the half million wasted in previous decades in order to keep the old structure on its feet.

The character of the bridge remained virtually unchanged for forty years. Although there is mention in the original construction documents of the provision of 'two tramways at the sides – of 7 feet 6 inches wide', this refers to sets of iron plates, which were bolted to wooden beams fixed in the roadway. They were designed to give a smoother ride for heavily laden carts and vans. Conventional horse drawn street tramways were banned from the bridge, and the authorities showed a similar lack of enthusiasm for a plan mooted in February 1898. It was suggested that the London Tramways Company should extend their cable system from the existing terminus at Brixton via a new route across Westminster Bridge and along the Embankment to Blackfriars.

It was not until 1906, when the LCC secured construction rights for tracks leading on to the Embankment, that electric tramcars were eventually able to cross the bridge. Alterations to the original structure entailed the raising of the bridge parapet plus the installation of cross bracing girders to support the two new tram tracks. The underground conduit method of current collection was employed, thus avoiding the use of overhead wires and traction standards across the bridge. The northernmost rail of the tramway was a mere two feet six inches (762mm) from the kerb. This created a situation whereby both tracks were offset well away from the centre of the carriageway.

The seemingly endless procession of trams added to the growing presence of motor vehicles. However, in spite of

The year is 1926 and the General Strike is over. Westminster Bridge is the setting for an overtly political gesture. The War Office has sent a detachment of the First Guards Brigade on a march through London. The soldiers, who had been quartered in Victoria Park, were originally posted to the docks in the East End. An inspector accompanies the motorman of the leading tram. Most LCC crews had taken part in the General Strike and we can only guess what the tram driver thought of all this pomp and circumstance in front of him. Perhaps the inspector was on board to stop him remonstrating with one of the mounted officers leading the armed column. Passions ran very high between the strikers and the forces of the state!

This is the bridge in the late 1930s. Groups of pedestrians have gathered to watch the loading of pleasure steamers at Westminster Pier. The buildings of St Thomas's Hospital dominate the Surrey side of the Thames. J.B.Gent Collection

continuing fears of subsidence affecting the bridge piers, the whole fabric of Westminster Bridge has proved more than equal to the task of coping with the ebb and flow of both water and road traffic. In 1924, a report commissioned by the LCC made the following observations:

The whole of the structure as it exists today is practically in as sound a condition as when it was constructed more than sixty years ago, largely due to the good design, to the excellent workmanship, to the high factor of safety adopted by the Engineer when he was considering the possible road load under conditions existing at the time the Bridge was designed, and also to the great care which has evidently been taken in its preservation.

Two years after the LCC report, the ROYAL COMMISSION ON CROSS-RIVER TRAFFIC IN LONDON delivered its findings. The Commission stated that London, Waterloo, Blackfriars, Westminster and Vauxhall bridges carried between them some sixty percent of all London's cross-river traffic. Westminster alone could claim a higher percentage of passenger and trade vehicles than any other bridge in the capital. A census recorded in July 1926 showed that, in a twelve hour period, no fewer than 19,365 vehicles crossed the bridge. This figure excluded trams. The Commission goes on to state:

The Ministry of Transport's view is, that while there is at present no congestion on the bridge itself, it is undesirable that the traffic should be seriously increased. There is little margin available, having regard to the frequent occasions when repairs to the road surface or the tramway track or openings for the other utility services, have to be made. Moreover, the approaches on the southern side are most unsatisfactory and their improvement would involve very heavy expenditure.

The approach from South London was via Westminster Bridge Road. This early 1950s scene depicts much that has been swept away in the intervening years. Note the war damaged buildings on the right. Tram 557 is about to enter the single track in York Road – part of the new layout constructed for the 1951 Festival of Britain. D.A.Thompson/LCCTT

Although the number of vehicles crossing the bridge in 1926 looks paltry to modern eyes, the comments about disruption caused by roadworks are bang up to date. The Commission also expressed a pious hope that the planned Charing Cross Bridge would alleviate the situation as far as Westminster was concerned. Unfortunately, subsequent events and the lack of money effectively torpedoed this suggestion. Major reconfiguration of approach roads on the Surrey side of the river had to wait until after the Second World War, although the Luftwaffe had already jumped the gun by starting the process of property demolition. Nazi bombs had obligingly removed a number of obstructions, including the well known Gatti's Palace of Varieties in Westminster Bridge Road. There was also extensive wartime damage in the York Road and Belvedere Road areas adjacent to the County Hall.

The task of easing the traffic flow on to the bridge from the South London approaches took another step forward in 1951, when a new road layout was constructed in advance of the Festival of Britain. Much to the joy of the small, but vocal, band of London tramway enthusiasts, several sections of tram track were installed to fit in with the revised one way gyratory system. Trams entering and leaving Westminster Bridge had full use of the improved facilities after 12th October 1950, by which time the first stage of the postwar tram to bus conversion had already taken place. This process was completed on 5th July 1952 and the rails across the bridge finally fell silent. When track removal took place in 1953/54, the whole carriageway was resurfaced in advance of promised further highway improvements connected with the eventual redevelopment of St Thomas's Hospital. However, these did not materialise for another two decades, by which time the volume of road users attempting to cross the bridge had reached proportions undreamt of by the 1926 Royal Commission.

Care of Westminster Bridge now partly rests with LoBeg (the London Bridges Engineering Group) – a consortium of London highway authorities, whose remit is to monitor and improve the capital's bridges. The complete structure belongs in a Grade II Listed Building category, and as such, merits very exacting

restoration work. A complete survey, carried out in 1989, resulted in an extensive renovation to ensure reliability well into the twenty-first century. The peak load is now around 3,000 vehicles per hour, plus the large numbers of pedestrians, who regularly use the bridge to get from the South Bank to Westminster and Whitehall.

This view is dated 22nd May 1948. The Thames is momentarily devoid of vessels and the only signs of life are the three trams crossing the bridge. B.T.Cooke

Midday on Saturday, 5th July 1952, and there is hardly a motor car, bus or lorry in sight. Perhaps this was a sympathetic response to the fact that this was the trams' final day. Electric traction took centre stage, with every single vehicle packed with passengers intent on taking just one last ride.

Chapter 8 WATERLOO BRIDGE

EVERY BRIDGE gains a reputation. Some bridges are destined to be feted by writers and artists, whilst others never seem to emerge from the relative obscurity of their utilitarian task of connecting point A with point B. The two river crossings bearing the name 'Waterloo' have attracted admiration and controversy in equal measure. Since the first decade of the nineteenth century, arguments have arisen over matters both sublime and ridiculous. The Waterloo bridges, in their time, have become a political football in a storm of debate. As with all tempests, the sound and fury have now abated, leaving a graceful modern structure, which is a credit to London.

Parliament was divided as to the need for a bridge linking the Strand with the South Bank of the Thames, but in spite of the doomsayers and critics, the first stone of the original structure, called Strand Bridge, was laid on 11th October 1811. The ceremonial opening took place on 18th June 1817. In the meantime, an Act of Parliament in 1816 had altered the name to Waterloo Bridge. George Dodd was the architect and John Rennie the guiding light behind the construction of the granite bridge, which spanned the Thames by means of nine arches. Two footways of 7 feet 6 inches (2.2 metres) each and a roadway of 27 feet 6 inches (8.3 metres) were provided. The

These elegantly dressed Londoners have paid their toll to cross the bridge and have stopped to admire the view. The date of this print is 1832, and the background scene already shows signs of the impact of the Industrial Revolution. Guildhall Library

This postcard scene dates from a century ago. An orderly stream of horse drawn vehicles is observed on Waterloo Bridge, while precious little seems to be happening on Victoria Embankment outside Somerset House. The skyline in those days was refreshingly devoid of tall office buildings.

latter could only cope with three lines of traffic, which put it at a disadvantage when compared to wider river crossings such as Westminster Bridge. The approach from the Strand to the bridge was 310 feet (94.4 metres); the bridge itself reached a length of 1,380 feet (420.6 metres), with a further 766 feet (233.4 metres) of causeway arches on the Surrey side.

Over a million pounds was sunk in the project – a vast sum for those days. The owning company was so optimistic in its forecasts that investors piled in, certain of profits to come. The directors pointed to the success of the nearby Westminster and Blackfriars bridges as a yardstick for the new enterprise. What they didn't emphasise was that everyone would have to pay a toll to use Waterloo Bridge, whereas all and sundry could saunter across the other two river crossings mentioned without having to put their hands in their pockets.

Quite predictably, Londoners with an eye to economy voted with their feet, and disappointment and frustration set in very quickly for the shareholders of the benighted company. The only silver lining in this very large cloud was that the number of people committing suicide by jumping off the bridge was considerably lower than at other locations by the Thames!

The tariff for traversing Waterloo Bridge contained varying charges and these might have appeared profitable to those investors unaware of the potential competition from the toll free river crossings. Pedestrians paid a penny to use the bridge, stagecoaches were charged a shilling each and omnibuses squeezed past for an outlay of sixpence. In 1840 the yearly sum raised by tolls reached a total of £13,535 – a good way short of expectations. The rot set in speedily, and by 1854, the company was acknowledged to be insolvent.

Fast tides scouring the riverbed were blamed for much of the damage to the piers of John Rennie's bridge. The back of this postcard is marked London Sept. 1924, and the printing on the front alludes to the repairs necessary to save the original Waterloo Bridge. An array of floating mechanical aids has been assembled in an (ultimately vain) attempt to shore up the structure. Since these works restricted navigation, it was always a worry for the authorities that a rogue vessel could strike one of the remaining arches and thus deliver the *coup de grace* to the bridge. J.B.Gent Collection

WATERLOO BRIDGE. SHOWING REPAIRS TO SAVE THE STRUCTURE.
57302.

The bridge was finally freed from tolls in 1878, by which time the annual income was hovering around the £22,000 mark. It is recorded that, in the year after crossing charges were lifted, some 6,657 vehicles per week were using the bridge, together with 24,253 pedestrians.

Horse bus operators were quick to spot the opportunity of running via Waterloo Bridge without paying the customary sixpence, thereby offering passengers a good choice of services from south London to the City and beyond. Parliamentary authority for a tramway was not forthcoming, and trams never got closer than the terminus in Waterloo Road just by the station. However, these vehicles did run under the bridge approach on the Middlesex side at Lancaster Place, this being the route of the Kingsway Tram Subway.

The abolition of tolls and the subsequent winding up of the bridge company might have heralded a more prosperous and secure era, but serious problems associated with subsidence began to surface. Work commenced in 1882 to reinforce the bridge piers and this continued for two years. This was only a partial solution, because movement of the bridge foundations was again confirmed in October 1923. From then on, the situation was under constant surveillance. On 11th May 1924, the bridge was closed to allow essential repairs to take place. At the same time, a temporary relief bridge was started alongside Rennie's masterpiece. The main focus of attention was the state of piers four and five – the eight piers were numbered from the Surrey side. It was reported that pier four had subsided some 28 inches (711mm) since 1820, and that the other seven had also deteriorated. Traffic was permitted back on the main bridge from July 1924, and the temporary bridge opened in the August of the following year.

Conjecture about the future fuelled the debate as to the

Our vantage point is on the South Bank of the river. We are looking across Waterloo Bridge to Somerset House on the Embankment. In the foreground is Bazon Street with an alleyway dividing Commercial Buildings. The tall chimney belongs to Waterloo Mill by Waterloo Bridge Wharf on Commercial Road. On the extreme left of the picture, behind the approaching motor bus, is a row of dwellings, which back on to Canterbury Wharf. Needless to say, the ravages of the Blitz and postwar planners have accounted for just about every structure on the Surrey side of the river. This scene today is quite unrecognisable.
J.B.Gent Collection

renovation of the structure. Unfortunately no one could agree exactly on a unified approach to reinforcing the foundations or to enlarging the carriageway in order to cope with the expected increase in traffic. The 1926 Royal Commission had this to say on the subject:

Various schemes have been submitted by eminent architects and engineers suggesting methods by which additional width for road traffic could be provided without adding to the length of the arch 'tunnels', but in none of these expedients has it be found possible to avoid some interference with Rennie's design. This we regard as regrettable, but the minimum needs of traffic must be met and we have come to the conclusion that the roadway of the bridge should be widened to 35 feet, in order to make it capable of taking four lines of vehicular traffic, whilst not diminishing the present width of the footways. The resulting addition to the load, both live and dead, on the new foundations of the bridge would almost be negligible and we are satisfied that the necessary widening could be effected without altering Rennie's design to any objectionable extent.

It has been submitted to us that such widening may be accompanied by moving the footways and the balustrades slightly away from the centre. This would necessarily affect the elevation as seen from the Embankment; but we are satisfied that it would be practicable to make the necessary modification of the upper course of Rennie's design without impairing the general effect and beauty of the bridge as seen from its neighbours, or its harmonious relation to Somerset House and St Paul's Cathedral.

The Commission's policy decision was backed up by submissions from several notable architects, all of whom were

This splendid picture was taken in August 1935. It shows demolition in progress on the old Waterloo Bridge. A cradle of steel girders, supported by jacks and reinforced bridge abutments, is being put in place. Its task is to transfer 9,000 tons of bridge weight from the existing nine arches. Meanwhile, back on Victoria Embankment life goes on as normal. The tram conductor doesn't even bother to glance up to see what's happening!
J.B.Gent Collection

ready to put forward their individual pet schemes to remedy the situation. Even the famous Sir Alexander Gibb entered the arena. Accompanied by Mr Humphreys, Chief Engineer of the LCC, he inspected the bridge in October 1926 and submitted his report shortly thereafter.

Throughout the Depression of 1929–1933 the status quo was maintained – no money could be found for capital works. However, those who wished to preserve John Rennie's handiwork were in for a severe shock, when, on 8th March 1934, the Labour Party swept to power in the London County Council elections. This was the first time in almost three decades that the radical left had been given a chance to implement its policies, and the opportunity was not missed to solve the stalemate concerning Waterloo Bridge. Very simply, it was going to be knocked down and a new one put in its place. This was entirely consistent with the view of the majority party that the

In the last month before the outbreak of the Second World War, an amateur photographer took this shot of work progressing on the new bridge. The project was slowed down by the war, and much of the labour was then entrusted to women workers, thus earning the new structure the soubriquet of the *Ladies' Bridge*. Note the Shot Tower to the right of the picture. James Whiting Collection

old fashioned forces of reaction had to be defeated across the metropolis. Some members at County Hall had brought back glowing reports of how the Russians set about town planning. If the Soviets could move whole streets in Moscow, then the London Labour Party should be able to tackle something as basic as a Thames bridge!

The colourful debate gets this succinct write up in a 1935 pamphlet, London under Socialist Rule, written by Herbert Morrison and D. H. Daines:

Although former (Tory) Councils had fooled with Waterloo Bridge for ten years, wasting about £100,000 in the process, the new Labour majority, within three months, came to a decision and put it into operation . . .

The bearers of the red flag did not mince words when it came to describing the lack of support from Whitehall:

. . . the Tory House of Commons rejected the Council's proposal, so that the Council has to find the money out of revenue; this the Finance Committee has arranged in a way which will involve no impossible burden to London, but the Ministry of Transport has refused to make any grant towards the cost.

Faced with this negative response from the Establishment, voices were raised in support of a name change for the bridge. Suggestions included 'Peoples Bridge' and 'Workers Bridge'; for a time, 'Peterloo Bridge' was a front runner amongst the radicals – this refers to the famous massacre of workers at St Peter's Fields, Manchester on 16th August 1819. In fairness to the decision makers at County Hall, they resisted the pressure to rename and, at the same time, they chose a splendid design for the new bridge.

Postcard views published during the war were often of mediocre quality. This particular example is included for its rarity value. The temporary river crossing is still in place, and will remain so for a few months, whilst the finishing touches are put to the new bridge. It would seem that only southbound traffic has been allowed on to the carriageway. Pedestrians have the option of traversing the structure in both directions. J.B.Gent Collection

The epithet 'graceful' is often applied to Waterloo Bridge. The elegant lines of the structure are apparent in this modern view, taken looking towards St Paul's and the City of London. R.J. Harley

Sir Giles Gilbert Scott (1880–1960) was commissioned by the London County Council to produce plans for the replacement. The bridge featured curved spans of reinforced concrete beams faced with Portland stone. Sir Giles was already known for a number of architectural successes, including his 1925 design for the standard GPO telephone kiosk, which is now famous the world over. He was also responsible for Battersea Power Station and the postwar rebuilding of Bankside Power Station, which now houses the Tate Gallery of Modern Art.

A symbolic removal of the first stone of the 1817 bridge took place in June 1934, with Herbert Morrison, Leader of the LCC, and G. Russell Strauss, Chairman of the Highways Committee, well to the fore. Demolition of the old stone structure also affected the southern portal of the Kingsway Tram Subway, which had to be reconstructed and the tracks realigned to fit under the new bridge. The original fifteen arch brickwork viaduct designed by John Rennie, which covered Lancaster Place Vaults, was retained as the northern approach to Waterloo Bridge.

The clash between the Labour controlled LCC, on one side of the river, and the Conservative Government, on the other, rumbled on for three years. The power and influence of those prominent citizens who wished to conserve John Rennie's bridge was not to be lightly underestimated. Finally, in December 1937, the Government relented and the Minister of Transport, Mr Leslie Burgin, announced a grant of 60 per cent towards the construction of the new Waterloo Bridge. Pointedly, he refrained from offering money from the exchequer to cover the cost of demolishing the old structure. This burden was to be borne by the ratepayers of London.

Construction work was severely curtailed by the outbreak of the Second World War and the whole project lasted from 1937 to 1944. The official foundation stone was laid in 1939, but thereafter progress continued steadily until 1942, when pedestrians and two lanes of traffic were allowed on to the structure. The full opening of the 80 feet (24.3 metres) wide and 1,250 feet (381 metres) long bridge had to wait until 1945.

The bridge has a shape and style that many photographers and artists have found attractive. In this it has inherited the tradition of John Rennie's bridge, which claimed the attention of Impressionist painters such as Claude Monet. Waterloo Bridge remains one of the most impressive of the Thames river crossings.

An imposing arch of Waterloo Bridge dwarfs a couple of midday joggers as they make their way along the Embankment.
R.J. Harley

Chapter 9 BLACKFRIARS BRIDGE

At THE northern end of the Embankment, just across the boundary dividing the City of Westminster from the City of London, lies the important river crossing of Blackfriars Bridge. London has a history of replacing its bridges on a regular basis, and in the case of Blackfriars, it was the usual story: the new ousted the old. Initially, it was suggested that the name William Pitt Bridge should be used, but political squabbling sabotaged this idea.

The Lord Mayor of London laid the foundation stone of the first structure on 31st October 1760, and building works were finished eight years later. The official inauguration of Blackfriars Bridge, designed by Robert Mylne, came on 19th November 1769. The new bridge of Portland stone was supported on nine elliptical arches, and the length was recorded as 995 feet (303.2 metres), with a 28 feet (8.5 metres) wide carriageway, flanked by two 7 feet (2.1 metres) wide footpaths. The total cost amounted exactly to £152,840 3s 10d, some of which was recouped by charging a toll of one halfpenny for every pedestrian – this was increased to a penny on Sundays. This set of charges was applied to every traveller, except during the Gordon Riots of 1780, when a mob wrecked the tollgates, assaulted the staff and then made off with the day's takings!

The opening of Blackfriars Bridge in November 1869 was a grand affair accompanied by all the necessary pomp and circumstance. This contemporary engraving depicts Queen Victoria and her entourage as the royal procession crosses the latest addition to London's river crossings. Wooden stands, erected for the convenience of the invited guests, have the effect of obscuring the parallel railway bridge.

Plan and elevation drawing of the widened bridge, dated 1909.

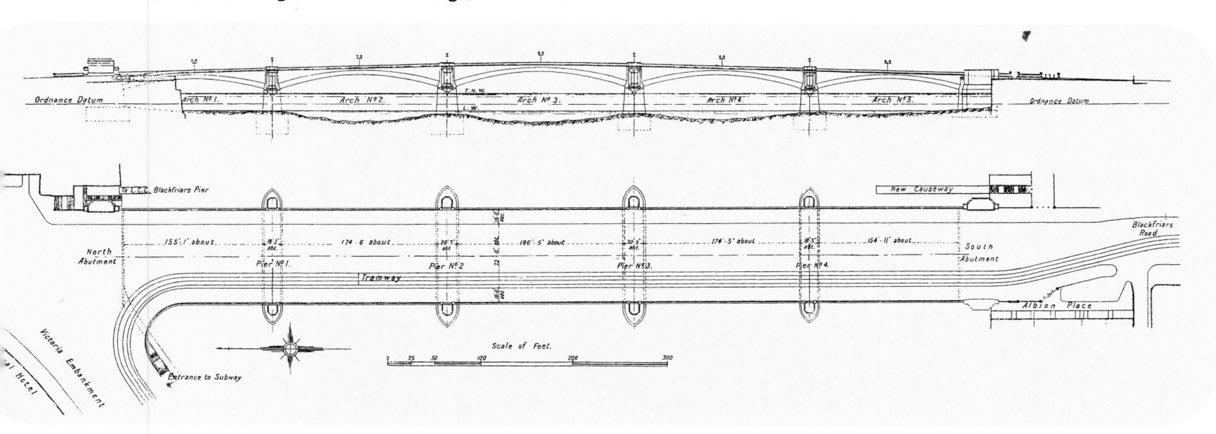

This map extract shows the contrast between the two banks of the Thames – wharves on the Surrey side and administrative buildings on the City side of the river. The original Blackfriars Pier and landing stage is situated in the narrow space between road and rail bridges.

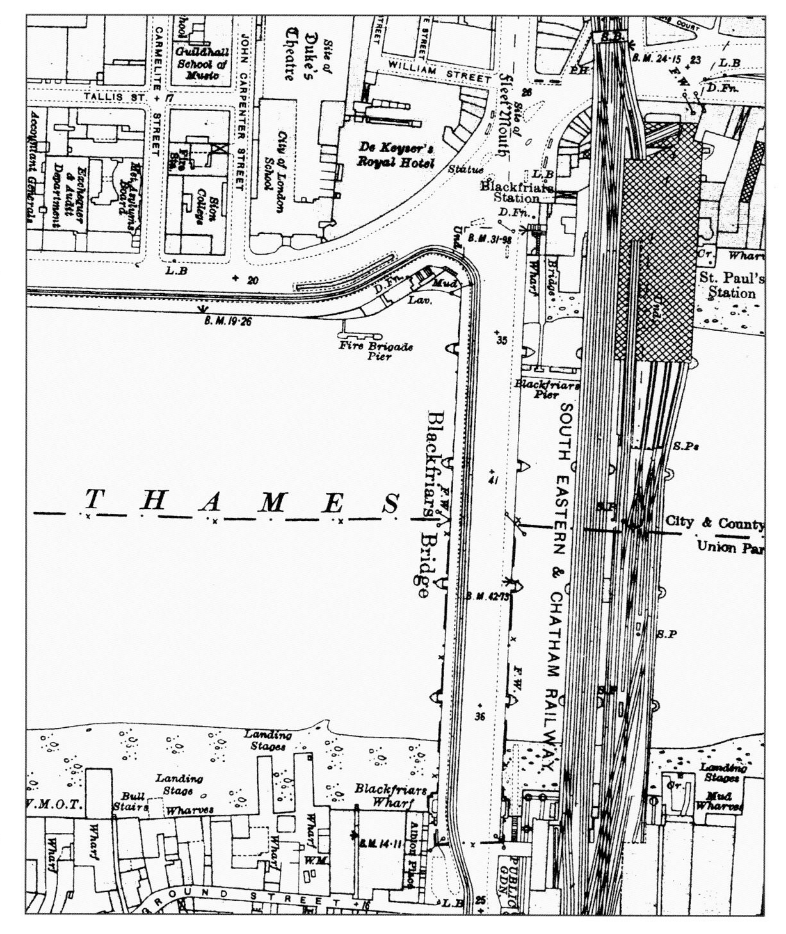

Suitable access roads were vital for the long term success of the project, and the construction of New Bridge Street bestowed another real benefit on Londoners. This piece of civil engineering involved the removal of an unsavoury area of slum dwellings; at the same time, the Fleet River was diverted to run in a culvert. On the South Bank, property demolition was kept to a minimum in the laying out of Albion Place (subsequently incorporated into Blackfriars Road) leading to St George's Circus.

Later modifications to the bridge itself included the lowering of the roadway and the footpaths, and the replacement of the open balustrade by a plain parapet. These building alterations were probably of less interest to the general public than the abolition of tolls, which occurred in June 1785. By the very nature of its location, the bridge attracted increasing traffic, which placed additional stresses and strains on the fabric of the structure. As with other bridges over the River Thames, subsidence and settling of the foundations soon became a major headache. The frequency of harsh winters did not help matters, and it was not unusual for the whole river to freeze over. On one particularly famous 'Frost Fair' in February 1814, market traders set up their stalls around the piers of the bridge, while the populus walked, skated or drove past!

Repairs to strengthen the piers were necessary between 1833 and 1840, but the work was only a stopgap until a larger, more durable bridge could be built. The decision to condemn the Mylne bridge was taken in 1863, and a temporary wooden structure was erected alongside. An account written in 1865 describes it as 'a timber viaduct, with three openings for the river navigation, each 70ft clear in the span, and supported by iron girders. The roadway for vehicles is carried along the top part of the bridge'. Provision was also made for pedestrians to use two gas lit walkways, which were positioned above the carriageway.

This artist's impression of the widened Blackfriars Bridge was published in the TRAMWAY & RAILWAY WORLD for 4th November 1909. The building sitting on the hill in the far distance is the Crystal Palace.

Construction work on the widening of Blackfriars Bridge is in full swing. This task was a prerequisite of the trams being granted access from St George's Circus to the Embankment, thus completing the great terminal loop. As was often the case throughout London, the tramway operator had to foot the bill for highway improvements, which benefited everyone – including the competing buses!

The engineering firm of Cubitt was commissioned to draw up plans for a bridge of five arches resting on granite piers. The main construction material was wrought iron faced with cast iron. Work started with the laying of the foundation stone on 20th July 1865. It was always intended that the new 1,272 feet (387.7 metres) long structure would be able to cope with the demand of cross river traffic, and with this in mind, the carriageway was widened to 80 feet (24.3 metres). The ceremonial opening by Queen Victoria took place on 6th November 1869.

Concurrent with the opening was the inauguration of the first section of Queen Victoria Street, which was projected to run from Mansion House to a junction with New Bridge Street. From January 1871, through traffic could use the new road to reach the City from Blackfriars Bridge. A few months later on the other side of the river, on 6th September, horse trams reached a terminus in Blackfriars Road. There the rails ended until large scale engineering works were carried out to enlarge Blackfriars Bridge. These were in connection with the extension of the LCC tramways from their temporary terminus by John Carpenter Street, on the Embankment, to complete 'the loop' with tracks leading to St George's Circus and the Elephant and Castle in south London.

The edition of TRAMWAY & RAILWAY WORLD for 4th November 1909 describes the events:

The work on Blackfriars Bridge was finished ahead of the three years' contract time . . . The Embankment line now forms an enormous loop, so that there is no terminus at the city end of the southern tramways. For several routes, at least, it is practicable for cars coming in by Blackfriars Bridge to return by Westminster Bridge and vice versa. The difficulty of finding a seat in a car at the busy hours of the evening has been largely overcome. The Embankment has, in fact, become a great loading and unloading ground for passengers, and the process is distributed along its length instead of being concentrated as formerly, at the termini.

The article goes on to chronicle the attempts by the LCC and their tramway predecessors to gain entry to the City of London by means of Blackfriars Bridge. All previous attempts had been rebuffed by the Corporation of the City of London. Their stance was based on the twin arguments that the streets of the City were too narrow for trams, and that the captains of commerce and banking didn't want them anyway. The inference here was that the tramcar was a vehicle for transporting the working classes and therefore had no place among the elite of the Empire – all pure snobbery, of course.

In a somewhat hypocritical gesture, bearing in mind the attitude of his wealthy colleagues, the Lord Mayor of London took the controls of the inaugural tram across the bridge. The date was 14th September 1909. The tracks from the Temple boundary to the southern end of the bridge were always owned by the City Corporation, but were leased to the London County Council. The total length of the new tramway brought into operation was 431 yards (131.3 metres).

For those interested in the technical aspects of the bridge widening, the TRAMWAY & RAILWAY WORLD has some detailed facts and figures, which characterise an era, when manual labour – pick and shovel work – was gradually being superseded by mechanical aids:

After reconstruction, the bridge still retained its graceful lines, as is evident in this picture, which was taken sometime around 1911.

Blackfriars Bridge is 922ft long between abutments and has five spans varying from 155ft to 185ft in length. Each of these is formed of arched ribs supporting the roadway girders. The width of the bridge between parapets was 75ft, and this is now increased to 105ft. Out of this, 73ft is given to the carriageway, and 16ft to each of the footpaths. The widening has been done by adding three additional plate girder ribs on the west side

The original fascia and parapet on that side have been moved outward and used again, so that the elevation appearance has not been changed except at the north end, where the west side sweeps on to the Embankment, so as to make a practical curve for the tramway.

In order to erect the additional superstructure, it was first necessary to lengthen the abutments and piers with their foundations in line with the river. Timber staging was erected in the Thames, and the foundations for the pier extensions were sunk by caissons. The caissons were

A new perspective – this time the tramlines are hidden, and we are greeted with the sight of an STL type bus on route 76. This was one of the standard workhorses of the LT Central Bus fleet during the thirties and forties, and examples could be seen in large numbers all over the metropolis. Route 76 traversed both Blackfriars and Westminster bridges on its way from Tottenham to Victoria.

We shift our observation spot to one of the parapets by Pier 3 of Blackfriars Bridge. The passengers on the top deck of LCC car 66 have a grandstand view of the Thames and of the Royal Hotel on the opposite bank.

shaped with a cut-water point, and with a recess at the other end to fit the point of the existing caissons. They were built over their final positions and then sunk, and subsequently the foundations were subjected to a test load of about 3,000 tons. The masonry of the piers is bonded to the original piers by steel girders.

To avoid the use of scaffolding above the water, the work of moving the existing face ribs 30ft outward was executed by means of an overhead traveller. This was carried on rails laid on the top of the new portion of each pier, and it was gradually moved forward, carrying the face girder, by means of tackle operated from cranes. The three new ribs were built into the space left between the old bridge and the face rib in its new position.

The double tram track was offset to the western side of the bridge, and other vehicular traffic generally steered clear of the tramlines. The inner rail was 3 feet 6 inches (1067mm) from the western kerb. Standard conduit components were used, and

A police notice warns road users to keep clear of the tram tracks, as tram and bus fight it out to see which one reaches the Blackfriars side first.
D.A.Thompson/LCCTT

Just past the southern approach to Blackfriars Bridge there was an important tramway junction, where routes serving the Borough and Hop Exchange diverged from the main tracks leading to St George's Circus. Unilever House is seen in the background, as car 1573 bears into Southwark Street.
D.A.Thompson/LCCTT

these were in line with similar LCC installations on Westminster and Vauxhall bridges. Very careful consideration was given to the construction of the elevated curves leading from the bridge on to Victoria Embankment. Part of this special trackwork was situated above a newly installed pedestrian subway. The reasons for its construction centred on the increased traffic at the intersection and the consequent problems for people trying to cross the road. The TRAMWAY & RAILWAY WORLD explains the situation:

The subway for foot passengers at the north end of the bridge is likely to be of great benefit to the public, as it underlies one of the most dangerous crossings in London. The former danger to pedestrians has been much aggravated since motor cars became common, and more especially since motor cabs began to dominate the Embankment. That broad thoroughfare is not much used by slow traffic, and it has become a sort of sprinting ground for motor vehicles travelling between the City and the West End.

Such were the portents for the future, and it was not unusual for drivers to come roaring along the Embankment, only to be pulled up sharply by slow moving carts and vans trying to leave the bridge. Accidents were giving cause for concern and the situation was partly remedied by the action described in the TWELFTH ANNUAL REPORT OF THE LONDON AND HOME COUNTIES TRAFFIC ADVISORY COMMITTEE 1936–1937:

The traffic signals which have been erected at the northern approach to Blackfriars Bridge and the eastern end of the Victoria Embankment do not regulate the movement of tramcars . . . To prevent other vehicular traffic, held up by the traffic lights, from cutting across the tram tracks, and thus creating conditions of danger, the Corporation of the City of London proposed that the use of the area occupied by the trams by vehicles other than trams should be prohibited.

We were consulted upon the proposal and whilst we are adverse to the creation of special privilege for any one class of vehicle on the highway, we advised you not to raise objection, as the circumstances are exceptional and the trams will probably be replaced by trolleybuses.

As it turned out, trolleybuses were fated never to run across Blackfriars Bridge – one suspects that the City authorities were much relieved when this decision was announced. The prospect of poles and overhead wires on the bridge was never very appealing. The trams hung on until the last day of operation in London. Removal of the tram rails enabled the whole road space to be used by motor traffic, the volume of which grew year on year. This great surge in vehicles throughout the sixties and seventies necessitated substantial highway alterations at the northern end of the bridge. A new underpass was built, which connected Victoria Embankment with Upper Thames Street. The latter, now officially recognised as an extension of the A3211, was totally reconstructed as a dual carriageway road leading past Cannon Street to emerge by Tower Hill. In theory, traffic could now avoid the congested central area and would have a straight run from Westminster to the Tower Gateway and beyond into the new Docklands developments of east London. In practice, the A201 Blackfriars Bridge now takes around 54,000 vehicles per day and many of these still get caught in slow moving columns of traffic. Trying to cross the road at the junction of the Embankment, New Bridge Street and Queen Victoria Street is a nightmare. It is still too early to say whether congestion charging will bring permanent

It is a fine summer's day in the mid 1930s and several familiar yellow Evening News vans are out delivering papers to newsstands. On the right, Unilever House and the neighbouring City of London School bask in the sunshine. A line of trams can be glimpsed along the Embankment, but there doesn't seem to be much activity on the steps of the subway leading to Queen Victoria Street and Blackfriars Pier.

relief to the area. Although not physically connected to the Embankment, it is worth saying a few words about the railway bridge adjacent to Blackfriars Bridge. The London, Chatham and Dover Railway Company's line from Herne Hill was extended, on 1st June 1864, from the Elephant and Castle to a terminus on the South Bank of the Thames. A new lattice girder bridge carrying lines to Ludgate Hill did not open until 21st December 1864. Work on the railway bridge was synchronised with the construction of the foundations for the second Blackfriars road bridge. For navigation purposes, the piers of the two neighbouring structures had to be in line. Passenger traffic increased, and a second railway bridge, leading to the new St Paul's Station (later renamed Blackfriars), was inaugurated on 10th May 1886. Both river crossings suffered damage in the Blitz, and the lattice girder bridge was later found to be suffering from corrosion. It was taken out of commission in June 1969 and was subsequently demolished in 1984.

This modern view shows clearly the renovated and repainted ironwork of Blackfriars Bridge. On the left of the picture is the landing stage of Blackfriars Millennium Pier. The Tate Gallery of Modern Art is featured in the background.

Chapter 10 CHARING CROSS BRIDGE

THE RAILWAY lines leading to Charing Cross Station were regarded by many as a blot on the landscape that was ripe for removal. The voices of the critics reached a crescendo in the late 1920s. Unfortunately, the debate sometimes deteriorated along class lines, with the well-to-do of the West End wanting to expel the railway and all its bag and baggage over to the poorer areas of the South Bank – 'out of sight, out of mind' seemed to be their motto. What was self evident, was that an elegant road bridge was to arise out of the ashes of the old South Eastern Railway Company structure.

In spite of the wartime emergency, several schemes were hatched in 1917 to remove Hungerford Bridge and replace it with a new structure solely for road traffic. The plan was conceived by W.D. Caroe, and was described thus:

It is a low level bridge running in line with Northumberland Avenue, and having a spur road from the Strand balancing Whitehall Place on the other side of Northumberland Avenue. It gives a very fine architectural arrangement at the Embankment, and an equally fine handling of the riverfront on the Surrey bank as far as Blackfriars Bridge. There is a curious twin arrangement of the two railway stations round a circle, with the front of Waterloo Station brought forward to the line of the circle, and St John's Church included in it. In this scheme by Mr Caroe, the tramway lines on the Embankment are lowered to pass under the bridgehead.

An idealised view of a late-1920s scheme devised by Thomas Collcutt. Note the rows of shops on the proposed bridge. Guildhall Library

Facing page **W.D. Caroe's 1917 scheme for the removal of Hungerford Bridge and re-siting of the South Eastern Railway terminus.**

MR COLLCUTT'S PROJECT FOR
STREET BRIDGES.
PROPOSED BRIDGE IN PLACE OF
CHARING CROSS RAILWAY BRIDGE
OR ON SOUTH SIDE OF SAME.

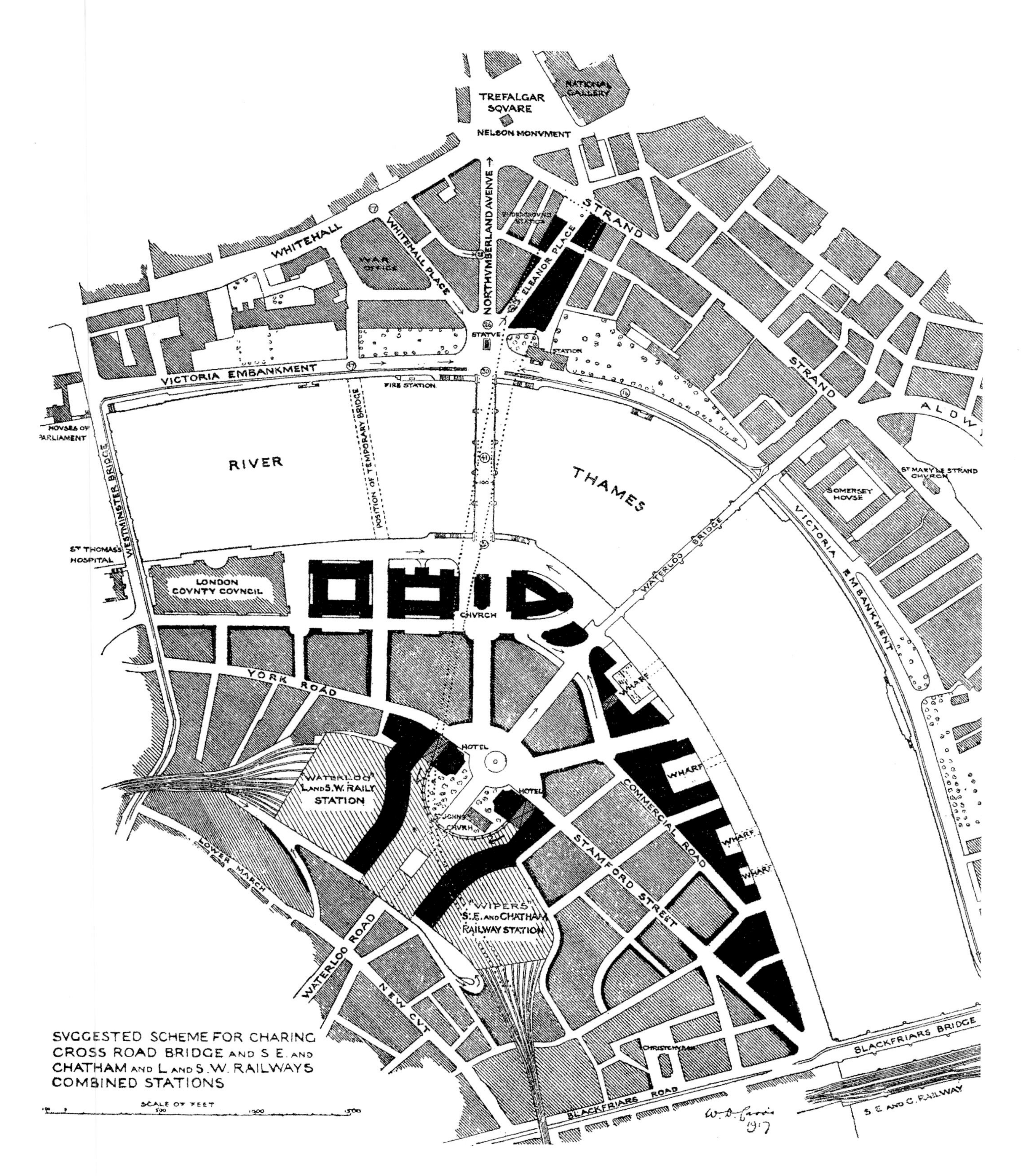

SVGGESTED SCHEME FOR CHARING CROSS ROAD BRIDGE AND S E. AND CHATHAM AND L AND S.W. RAILWAYS COMBINED STATIONS

This wonderfully detailed map was appended to the official 1926 report on cross river communications in London. What is proposed here is a new double deck bridge that would cater for both road and rail traffic. The scheme would have involved repositioning Charing Cross Station under the roadway leading to a junction with St Martin's Place. Care was also to be taken when excavating the riverbed because of the proximity of tube railway tunnels. The existing Hungerford Bridge would have been torn down – whether its planned replacement would have looked any more attractive is a matter for conjecture.

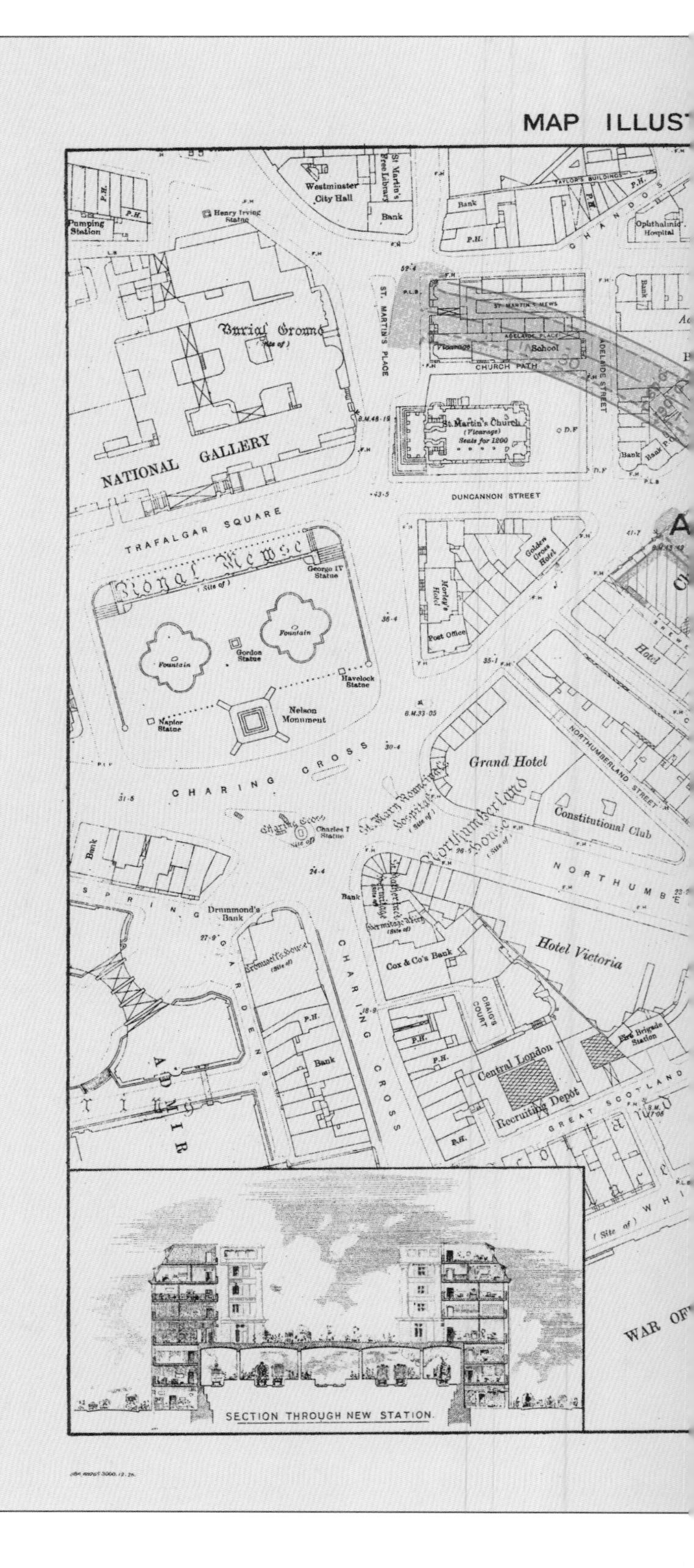

The 1926 Royal Commission, which put forward a number of cogent points in favour of the new bridge, also discussed the matter. A low level river crossing that would intersect the Embankment looked a possibility, as did a double deck structure. This latter had the merit of retaining the railway into Charing Cross, whereas the other schemes envisaged the replacement of the station by a large road junction with the Strand, which would involve a traffic roundabout and expensive property demolition.

Whichever way the critics of Hungerford Bridge looked, they could not just dismiss the usefulness of Charing Cross Station and wish it away from the scene. An alternative site for the London terminus of the North Kent lines would have to be found on the South Bank. The Commission argued the pros and cons, and eventually concluded:

. . . we desire to add that, in our view, a properly designed double deck bridge at Charing Cross can be made attractive to the eye and architecturally in harmony with its surroundings.

The Commission's Report also contains some very interesting memoranda on the subject of the Charing Cross Bridge. Several letters from the Southern Railway company are quoted in detail, and the impression they give is that no objection would be offered by the management to a new double deck bridge, constructed on the down-river side of the existing structure. It is also understood that any remodelling of Charing Cross Station would entail the complete elimination of steam locomotives. Maybe there was a hope here that the government would foot the bill for more electrification schemes.

As regards the effect of the proposal on Underground railways, the following section is very informative:

Any new bridge over the river at this crossing must avoid as far as river piers are concerned, any interference with the existing tube railways . . . In the river the top of the tube is approximately within 10 feet of the bed of the river, whilst at the embankments the top of the tube is 35 feet below the level of the Embankment.

There the matter rested, as regards officialdom, but this lack of action failed to dampen the speculation. Rational discussion of all the aspects of the problem was at a premium, but common sense did surface in a number of pamphlets and publications. One of the most interesting of these was Arthur Keen's work, entitled CHARING CROSS BRIDGE, which was published in 1930. The author covers at length many of the proposals for speeding up traffic and for improving the riverside vista from Westminster Bridge to St Paul's Cathedral.

APPENDIX 9.
PROPOSED CHARING CROSS BRIDGE SCHEME (NORTH SIDE)

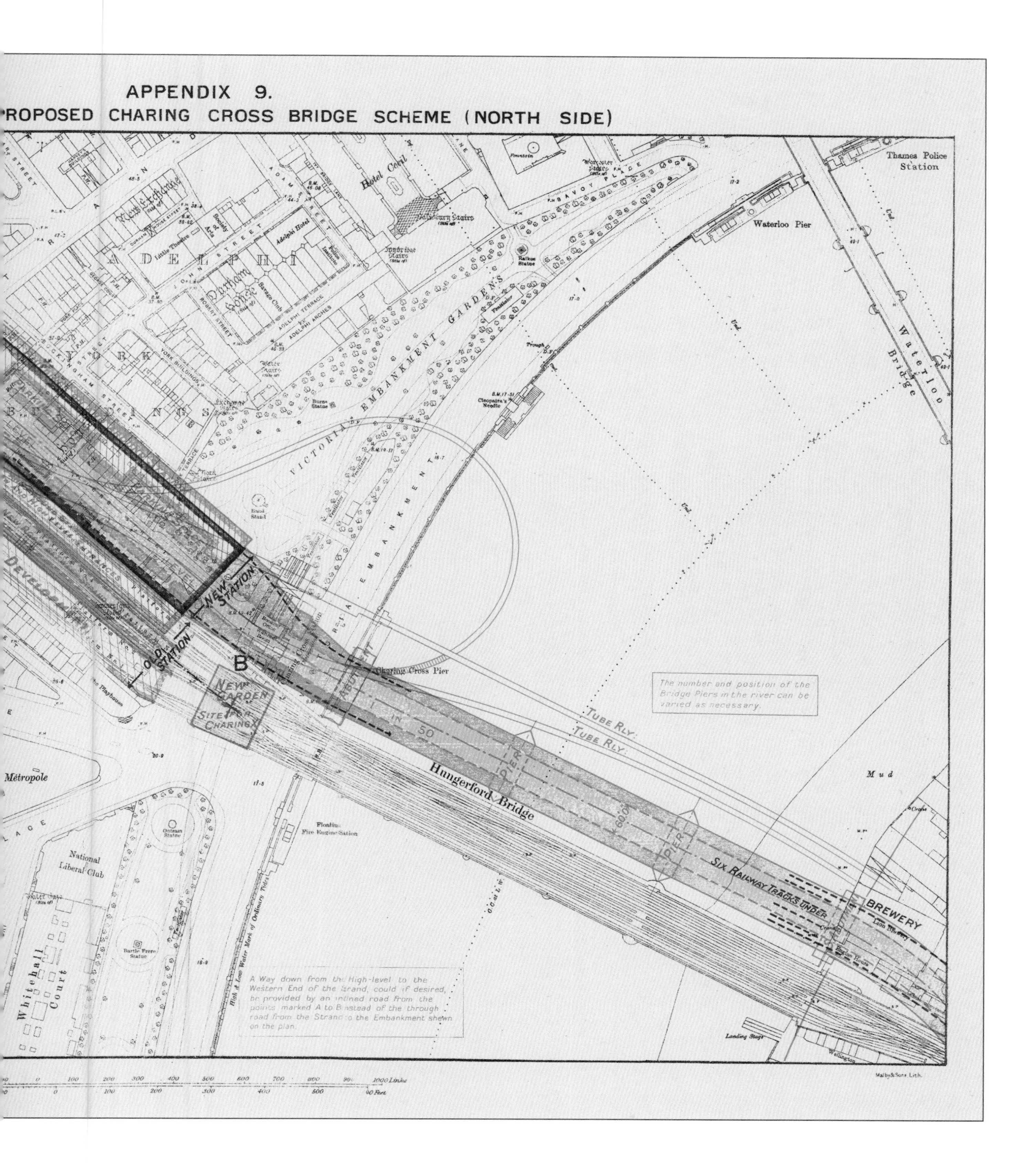

The designer of this scheme, published as one of a number of suggestions in the 1930 book entitled CHARING CROSS BRIDGE, saw knocking down Charing Cross Station and consigning Hungerford Bridge to the scrap heap as only a first step to a system of new roads and subterranean main line railways. The former railway alignment from London Bridge to Waterloo and Charing Cross would be converted to a 'High Level Fast Motor Road' – the 1930 equivalent of an urban motorway. The proposed Temple Bridge would further dissect Victoria Embankment. There are some quite workable ideas here, such as the waterbus service connecting the Thames piers, but the general impression is one of total capitulation to the motor car.

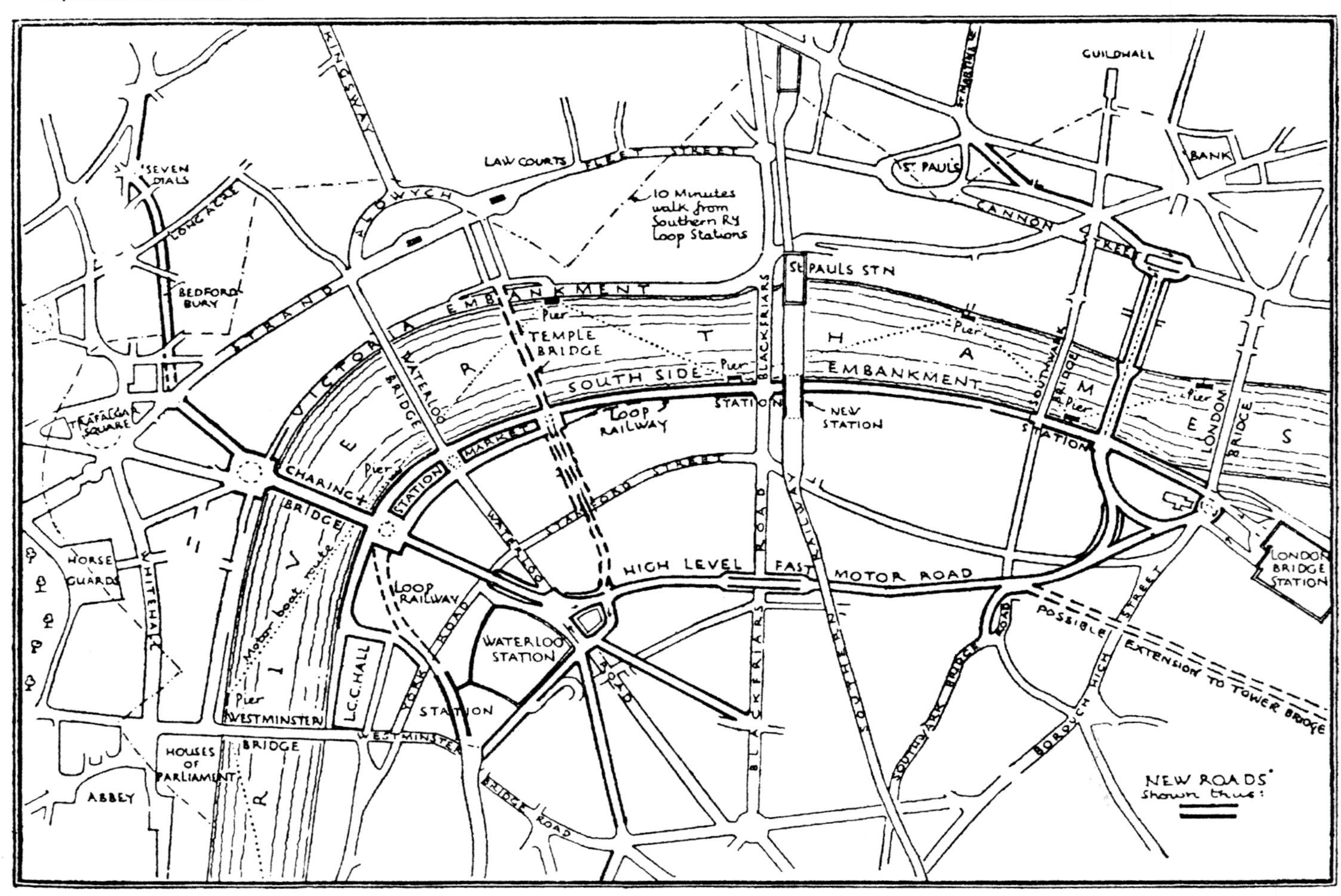

One concern of the time was to renovate the South Bank, so that it could present a 'mirror image' of the Victoria Embankment on the other side of the river. This particular transformation was delayed by the war and would have to wait until the 1951 Festival of Britain supplied the impetus for future developments.

Shortly before the Charing Cross Bridge book was published, the LCC had deposited plans for an imaginative scheme to solve the problem of easier cross river access to Charing Cross. Unsurprisingly, the whole effort was known as the 'official scheme' and can be seen on the map on page 115.

Noteworthy features included expanding the existing Waterloo Station into a much larger terminus and creating a new road embankment linking Waterloo Bridge with the northern boundary of County Hall near York Road. On the Westminster bank of the Thames, it was not envisaged that there would be any direct road connection with the Victoria Embankment. In fact all traffic would feed into a large roundabout planted on the forecourt of the former Charing Cross Station. Another roundabout, this time including the Waterloo Road tramway, was proposed for the eastern end of the new highway, just by the entrance to Waterloo Station.

As might be expected, what seemed a good idea in the smoke filled rooms of County Hall, began to unravel quickly in the face of stiff opposition. All kinds of faults were found, even before The House of Commons had had the chance to debate the

The LCC was nothing if not optimistic, when the planning department thought up this submission for the 1929-30 Parliamentary session. Note the idea of moving Charing Cross Station – lock, stock and barrel – over to the South Bank. Suspiciously, there are no tramways marked for Westminster Bridge Road and Victoria Embankment, but a revised track layout for Waterloo Road (terminus of route 68) has been included. It is safe to say that financial concerns caused by the worldwide trade depression helped to kill this one off.

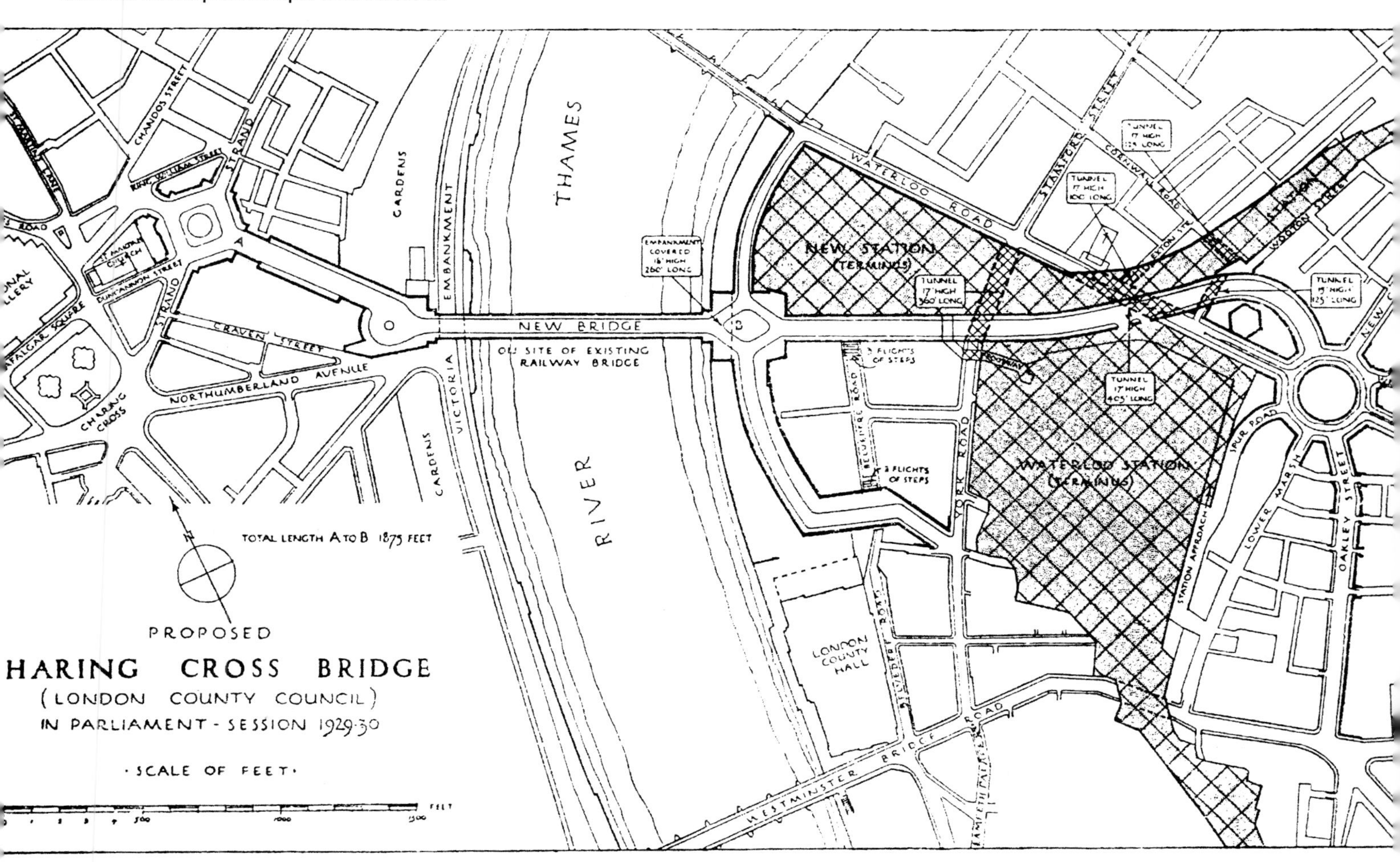

matter. It was pointed out that to 'dump' all the traffic on the congested Strand area was unrealistic, as was the lack of access from the Embankment. Vehicles coming along Victoria Embankment would be forced into a circuitous journey via Northumberland Avenue, Trafalgar Square and the Strand, to reach the bridge.

The Bill passed the House of Commons on 19th February 1930, but failed in the Committee Stage. Although MPs were favourable to many aspects of the scheme, the majority on the Committee did not believe plans for the South Bank had been sufficiently thought out. An adjournment was called so that all parties could consider an alternative site for the rail terminus, and with this, the whole grand scheme passed into limbo.

There then followed a glut of proposals springing up from all sides – the Lambeth Borough Council, professional architects, sundry town planners and interested members of the public. Newspaper correspondence columns were full of helpful suggestions, and older ideas, sometimes dating back to before the First World War, were revamped and thrown into the frame. However, as the castles in the air became more elaborate, so the projected costs started to spiral. If this hurdle could be surmounted, it seemed the possibilities were endless. Once the railway and Hungerford Bridge were removed, then underground loops for main line trains, elevated highways, a double width Victoria Embankment with a separate underpass for the trams, and many other modern designs could be considered.

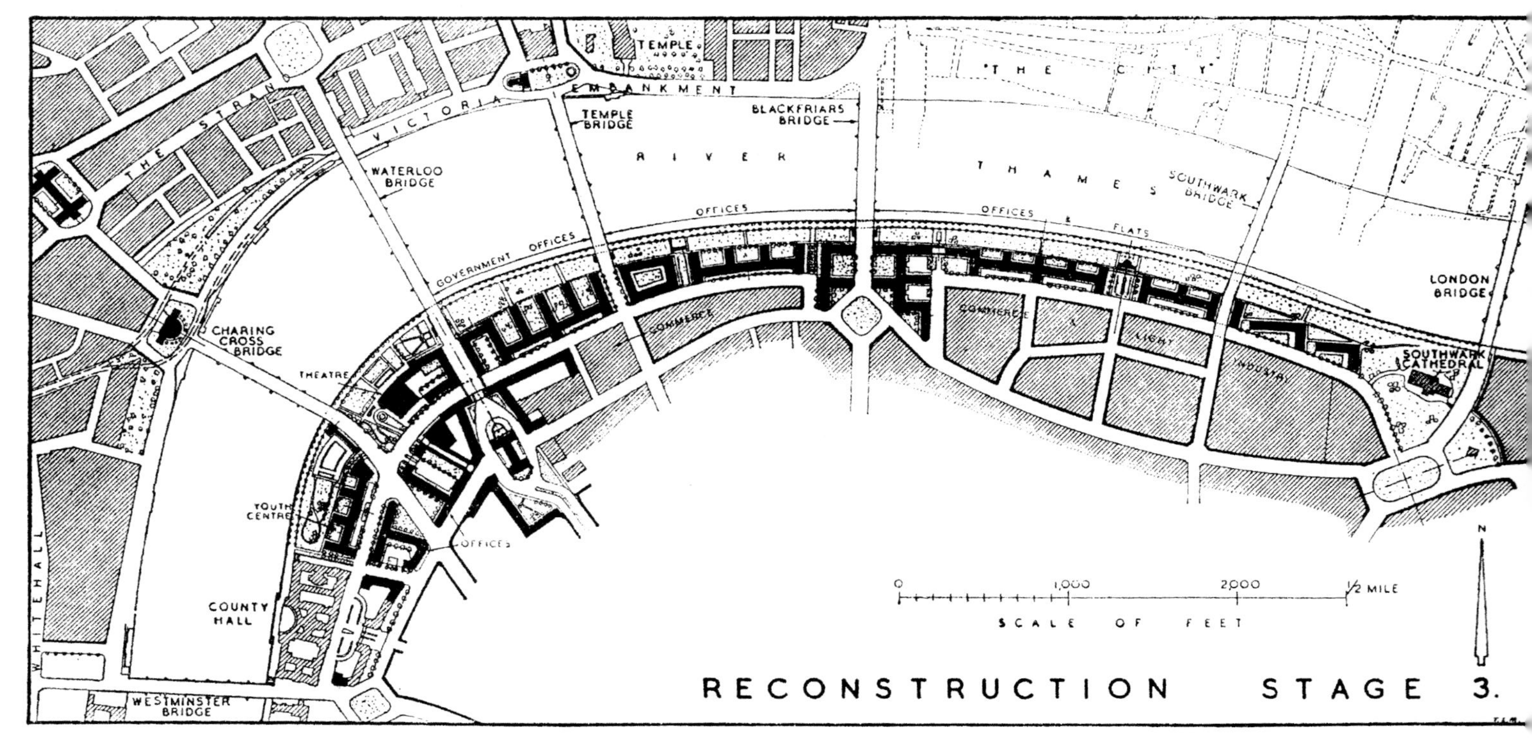

The authors of the County of London Plan 1943 suggested rearrangement of roads, bridges and river crossings to cope with the traffic pressures of the brave new postwar world. This map depicts the final stage of the proposal – stages one and two involved much demolition on the South Bank and the complete reconstruction of Victoria Embankment between Waterloo Bridge and the new Charing Cross Bridge. The idea for a Temple Bridge makes a reappearance.

Further plans for the Embankment area were formulated in the County of London Plan by J. H. Forshaw and Patrick Abercrombie, which was published in 1943. This comprehensive document, prepared for the London County Council, makes interesting reading, especially with regard to proposals for the postwar transport system of the metropolis.

Improvements suggested include the reappearance of the underground railway loop plan, which would render redundant not only Charing Cross Station, but also Blackfriars and Cannon Street as well. The Reconstruction Stage 3 scheme shows Victoria Embankment split into distinct sections. At Charing Cross, by the new bridge, there would be road subways feeding traffic away from the Thames in the direction of Whitehall. These were part of a new subterranean highway, which was destined to emerge into the open by a new arterial road in the Victoria area. The route formed a section of a proposed Tilbury to Portsmouth motorway that would be carried on a riverside embankment under Blackfriars Bridge and then onwards, right through the City of London.

Yet another new river crossing, named Temple Bridge, would intersect the Embankment, thereby creating a large traffic roundabout. At the Westminster end of the Embankment, another gyratory system was planned, which would have involved considerable property demolition between the southern part of Whitehall and the approach to Westminster Bridge. No thought was given to altering tram tracks, because by this time, electric vehicles tied to fixed rails were officially regarded as outdated.

Although everything seemed to be tailored to the needs of motor vehicles, a novel alternative to underground railway terminals was mooted in the form of buildings with 'flat roofs for future air landing' – obviously, the idea of people flying about in their own personal helicopters was still in the minds of those, who hadn't quite forgotten H. G. Wells's vision of the future!

Whatever happened to all these wonderful ideas? Nearly all of them vanished in the harsh light of postwar economic conditions, when the country was practically bankrupt and could not afford lavish construction projects. Austerity led predictably to 'make do and mend', and true to this philosophy, most of the road improvements over the past half century have been in the nature of piecemeal additions to the network. The basic layout of the Embankment and the connecting Thames bridges has remained more or less unaltered since the opening of Waterloo Bridge just after the end of the Second World War.

The new Hungerford footbridge partly obscures the railway bridge from the east. The London Eye towers above both.

INDEX

Index of People

General Text Index

SELECT BIBLIOGRAPHY

Researchers into Victorian London can call on a rich source of archive materials and books to assist them. Almost all aspects of the capital's social and economic life have been covered in detail. When preparing the present work, I have consulted *London: A Social History* by Roy Porter, *London: The Biography* by Peter Ackroyd, and Stephen Inwood's *A History of London*. *The History of the London County Council 1889-1939* by Sir Gwilym Gibbon and Reginald W. Bell gives an excellent overview of the era. Another 'period' contribution, which offers a very readable account of the streets and buildings of the metropolis, is Harold P. Clunn's *The Face of London*, first published in 1932.

The subject of the Thames bridges and embankments has been tackled in several publications. A painstaking study, which appeared in 1998, is Dale H. Porter's *The Thames Embankment*. It is packed full of interesting information and contains useful insights into the politics behind the construction of Victoria Embankment. *The Great Stink of London* by Stephen Halliday, published in 1999, describes the creative influence of Sir Joseph Bazalgette on the cleansing of the Victorian metropolis.

Patricia Pierce's book *Old London Bridge* is invaluable in detailing the life of the river. A good account of the great variety of river vessels employed on the Thames can be found in Frank Burtt's *Steamers of The Thames and Medway*, which was first published in 1949 and subsequently reissued in 1997. A comprehensive photographic album featuring river craft and riverbank scenes is Stephen Croad's *Liquid History – The Thames Through Time*, which was published by English Heritage in 2003.

The background to the tramways on the Embankment is detailed in *LCC Electric Tramways* published by Capital Transport in 2002, and *Embankment and Waterloo Tramways*, released by Middleton Press in 1994 – both books are by the present author.

Official reports consulted in the preparation of this book include the *Royal Commission on Cross-River Traffic in London*, dated 30th November 1926, and several annual submissions from the Ministry of Transport's London and Home Counties Traffic Advisory Committee. The 1943 *County of London Plan* by J.H. Forshaw and Patrick Abercrombie proposes many solutions for postwar reconstruction. Other unfulfilled plans for the future appear in the 1930 edition of *Charing Cross Bridge* by Arthur Keen, and in *London – Her Traffic – Her Improvement* by Captain George S.C. Swinton, which was published in 1924.